D1824218

SIDE DISHES
COOKBOOK

25 + Appetizers, Sides, Dishes and Desserts That Your Family Will Love

(A Yummy Corn Side Dish Cookbook You Will Love)

Brian Leslie

Published by Alex Howard

Side Dishes Cookbook: 25 + Appetizers, Sides, Dishes and Desserts That Your Family Will Love (A Yummy Corn Side Dish Cookbook You Will Love)

ISBN 978-1-990169-72-4

Legal & Disclaimer

The information contained in this book is not designed to replace or take the place of any form of medicine or professional medical advice. The information in this book has been provided for educational and entertainment purposes only.

Table of contents

Part 1

Peas, Pimento, And Pickled Relish

Prep Time: 20 mins

Total Time: 4 hrs 50 mins

Rice

Servings per Recipe: 8

Calories

424 kcal

Fat

26.2 g

Carbohydrates 30.1g

Protein

17.2 g

Cholesterol

159 mg

Sodium

691 mg

Ingredients

2 C. water

1 tbsp lemon juice

1 C. white rice

1/4 C. sweet pickle relish

6 eggs

1 (9 oz.) can solid white tuna packed in water,

1 (10 oz.) package frozen peas, thawed

drained

1 C. diced celery

1/4 tsp dried dill weed

1/4 C. diced onion

1 tsp salt

1 (4 oz.) jar minced pimento

1/8 tsp pepper

1 C. mayonnaise

1 tsp prepared mustard

Directions

1. Add your rice and some water to a big pot. Get everything to a rolling boil. Once boiling lower the heat. Place a lid on the pot

and let the rice cook for 22 mins. Then turn off the heat once the rice is tender.

2. Get a 2nd pot. Put your eggs in the pot and add enough cold water to submerge the eggs.

Get the water and eggs boiling. Then turn off the heat.

3. For 14 mins let the eggs sit in the water to cook. Remove the shells and dice the eggs.

4. Clean your peas then get a bowl.

5. Put the following in the bowl and evenly mix: pimiento, eggs, onions, rice, and celery.

6. Get a 2nd bowl, mix: pepper, mayo, salt, mustard, dill, lemon juice, tuna, and relish.

7. Combine both bowls, and evenly mix them. Then chill the mixture in the fridge for 5

hours.

8. Enjoy cold.

Peas, Pimento, and Pickled Relish Rice

9

Long Grain Chicken Flavored

Prep Time: 10 mins

Total Time: 35 mins

Chili Rice

Servings per Recipe: 6

Calories

83 kcal

Fat

2.6 g

Carbohydrates 13g

Protein

1.9 g

Cholesterol

2 mg

Sodium

757 mg

Ingredients

1 tbsp vegetable oil

1 tsp ground black pepper

1 C. long-grain white rice

2 C. chicken broth

1 (4 oz.) can diced green chilies

Directions

1. Get a frying pan hot with veggie oil. Add into the hot oil your chili peppers, and rice.

2. Stir fry the rice and peppers for 4 mins to get everything lightly coated and nicely toasted.

3. Add in your broth to the peppers, and heat the broth until it is boiling.

4. Lower the heat under the pan, place a lid on it, and cook for 22 mins. After the cooking time has elapsed your rice should be tender.

5. Enjoy warm.

12 Long Grain Chicken Flavored Chili Rice

Curry Rice

Prep Time: 5 mins

Total Time: 1 hr 10 mins

Servings per Recipe: 4

Calories

271 kcal

Fat

5.2 g

Carbohydrates 48g

Protein

8.1 g

Cholesterol

13 mg

Sodium

76 mg

Ingredients

1 C. jasmine rice

4 fresh curry leaves

2 C. water

1 pinch asafoetida powder (optional)

1 tbsp ghee (clarified butter)

1/4 C. milk

1 dried red chili pepper, broken in half

1 C. plain yogurt

(optional)

salt to taste

1 tsp black mustard seeds

1/2 tsp ground turmeric

Directions

1. Get a large pot and add in your rice and cover it with water. Bring the water to a rolling boil. Then set the heat to low. Place a lid on the pot and let the rice cook for 22 mins until soft.

2. Get a frying pan and stir fry your chili in ghee for 1 min. Then add in mustard seeds, and cook for another 1 min. Turn off the heat.

3. Add in your asafoetida powder, curry leaves, and turmeric spice to your peppers.

4. Get a bowl, mix: spicy peppers, yogurt and milk.

5. Combine the peppers with the rice and add some salt for seasoning.

6. Enjoy at room temp.

Curry Rice

13

South Of The Border Style Rice

Prep Time: 20 mins

Total Time: 55 mins

Servings per Recipe: 6

Calories

510 kcal

Fat

18.3 g

Carbohydrates 59.1g

Protein

28.3 g

Cholesterol

74 mg

Sodium

1294 mg

Ingredients

1 lb lean ground beef

1/2 tsp paprika

1 onion, minced

1/2 tsp garlic powder

1 green bell pepper, minced

1/2 tsp salt

1 (14 oz.) can beef broth

1/2 tsp ground black pepper

2 C. fresh corn kernels

1 tsp minced cilantro

1 (10 oz.) can minced tomatoes with

1 1/2 C. uncooked white rice

green chili peppers

1 C. shredded Cheddar cheese

1 (15 oz.) can tomato sauce

1/2 C. salsa

1/2 tsp chili powder

Directions

1. Fry your beef until fully done. Remove any excess oils or fats. Then mix in your green pepper, and onions.

2. Continue frying until the onions are soft. Add in your tomato sauce, beef broth, chili peppers with tomatoes, and the corn.

3. Heat this up for 2 mins.

4. Then mix in: cilantro, salsa, chili powder, pepper, paprika, salt, and garlic powder. Combine these contents evenly.

5. Then get everything boiling. Once boiling add in your rice.

6. Lower the heat. Place a lid on the pot and cook the rice for 26 mins until tender.

7. After 26 min add some cheddar and cook for another 10 mins.

8. Enjoy.

14

South of the Border Style Rice

Rice Dessert

Prep Time: 25 mins

Total Time: 45 mins

Servings per Recipe: 4

Calories

366 kcal

Fat

6.9 g

Carbohydrates 67.6g

Protein

8.8 g

Cholesterol

64 mg

Sodium

237 mg

Ingredients

3/4 C. uncooked white rice

2/3 C. golden raisins

2 C. milk, divided

1 tbsp butter

1/3 C. white sugar

1/2 tsp vanilla extract

1/4 tsp salt

1 egg, beaten

Directions

1. Get a saucepan add in your rice, and also 1.5 C. of water.

2. Bring everything to a rolling boil. Once boiling set the heat to low. Place a lid on the pot and let the rice cook for 22 mins.

3. Get a 2nd pot, combine in it: salt, 1.5 C. cooked rice, sugar, and 1.5 C. milk.

4. Heat this mix until it gets smooth and cream-like. This should take about 22 mins of cooking and occasional stirring.

5. Finally add in: raisins, the rest of your milk, and whisked eggs.

6. Heat for another 4 mins. Make sure to keep stirring.

7. Add in some vanilla and butter. And let the contents cool before serving.

Rice Dessert

15

Cashew Pilaf

Prep Time: 15 mins

Total Time: 40 mins

Servings per Recipe: 6

Calories 349

Fat 8.6

Carbohydrates 2

Protein 265

Cholesterol 59.5

Sodium 8.2

Ingredients

4 C. water

1/4 C. fresh lime juice

2 C. long grain rice, rinsed and drained

2 tbsp tamarind paste

1/2 tsp salt

1 C. plain yogurt

2 tbsp vegetable oil, divided

1/4 C. coarsely chopped cashews

7 small dried chile peppers

1 tsp mustard seed

1 tsp cumin seed

10 fresh curry leaves

1 tsp ground turmeric

Directions

1. In a pot, add the water and cook until boiling. Add the salt and rice and stir to combine. Set the heat to low and with a id cover the pan.

2. Cook for about 20-22 minutes.

3. Meanwhile, in a frying pan, add 1/2 tbsp of the oil over medium heat and cook until heated. Stir in the cashews and cook for 5 minutes. Transfer the cashews into a bowl and keep aside.

4. In the frying pan, add the remaining oil over medium heat and cook until heated.

5. Stir in the cumin seeds, mustard seeds and chile peppers and stir fry for about 30 seconds.

6. Stir in 1/2 of the cashews and curry leaves and stir fry for about 3 minutes.

7. Remove the rice from the heat and stir in the tamarind paste, lime juice and turmeric.

8. Now, place onto a platter and stir in the oil mixture.

9. Serve with a garnishing of the remaining cashews.

16

Cashew Pilaf

Louisiana Rice

Prep Time: 15 mins

Total Time: 50 mins

Servings per Recipe: 8

Calories

485 kcal

Fat

23.5 g

Carbohydrates 41.4g

Protein

26.2 g

Cholesterol

72 mg

Sodium

1541 mg

Ingredients

1 lb lean ground beef

1 (10 oz.) can diced tomatoes with green chili

1 lb beef sausage

peppers

1 onion, finely minced

2 (15 oz.) cans kidney beans, drained

1 (8 oz.) package dirty rice mix

salt and pepper to taste

2 C. water

Directions

1. Stir fry your onions, sausage, and beef. Until the meats are fully cooked. Remove any excess oils.

2. Get a saucepan and add in your water and rice along with: kidney beans, chilies and tomatoes.

3. Heat everything with high heat until boiling, then add in your meats and onions.

4. Get everything boiling again. Then combine in some pepper and salt.

5. Place a lid on the pan and set the heat to low and cook for 27 mins until the rice is nice and soft.

6. Fluff the rice and enjoy.

Louisiana Rice

17

Mumbai Yellow Rice

Prep Time: 5 mins

Total Time: 25 mins

Servings per Recipe: 6

Calories 154

Fat 4.1

Carbohydrates 10

Protein 418

Cholesterol 26.1

Sodium 2.5

Ingredients

1/8 tsp powdered saffron

1 C. uncooked long-grain white rice

2 C. boiling water, divided

1 tsp salt

2 tbsp butter

Directions

1. In a bowl, add 1/2 C. of the hot water and saffron and stir until well combined.

2. Keep aside for about 15-20 minutes.

3. Add the butter in a pan over medium-high heat and heat until melted completely.

4. Add the rice with salt and stir fry until aromatic.

5. Add the saffron water and remaining hot water and cover the pan.

6. Now, set the heat to low and simmer for about 20-25 minutes.

18

Mumbai Yellow Rice

How To Make Basmati Rice

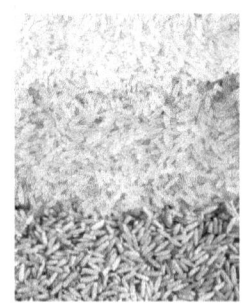

Prep Time: 10 mins

Total Time: 45 mins

Servings per Recipe: 6

Calories 216

Fat 5.4

Carbohydrates 0

Protein 394

Cholesterol 38.9

Sodium 3.9

Ingredients

1 1/2 C. basmati rice

1 tbsp cumin seed

2 tbsp vegetable oil

1 tsp salt

1 (2 inch) piece cinnamon stick

2 1/2 C. water

2 pods green cardamom

1 small onion, thinly sliced

2 whole cloves

Directions

1. In a large bowl of water, soak the rice for at least 25-30 minutes.

2. In a pan, add the oil over medium heat and cook until heated completely.

3. Stir in the whole spices and sauté for about 1 minute.

4. In the pan, add the onion and cook for about 10 minutes, stirring frequently.

5. Strain the soaked rice completely.

6. In the pan, add the strained rice and stir fry for about 1-2 minutes.

7. Stir in the water alongside the salt and let the mixture cook until boiling.

8. Now, set the heat to low and cook, covered for about 15-20 minutes.

9. Remove from the heat and keep aide, covered for about 5 minutes.

10. Uncover the pan and with a fork, gently fluff the rice.

11. Serve immediately.

How to Make Basmati Rice

19

Indo-Asian Chicken And Rice

Prep Time: 30 mins

Total Time: 2 hrs 30 mins

Servings per Recipe: 8

Calories

832 kcal

Carbohydrates

78.9 g

Cholesterol

134 mg

Fat

35.1 g

Protein

47.8 g

Sodium

1522 mg

Ingredients

4 tbsps vegetable oil

3 pounds boneless, skinless chicken

4 small potatoes, peeled and halved

pieces cut into chunks

2 large onions, finely chopped

2 1/2 tbsps vegetable oil

2 cloves garlic, minced

1large onion, diced

1 tbsp minced fresh ginger root

1pinch powdered saffron

1/2 tsp chili powder

5 pods cardamom

1/2 tsp ground black pepper

3 whole cloves

1/2 tsp ground turmeric

1(1inch) piece cinnamon stick

1 tsp ground cumin

1/2 tsp ground ginger

1 tsp salt

1pound basmati rice

2 medium tomatoes, peeled and

4 cups chicken stock

chopped

11/2 tsps salt

2 tbsps plain yogurt

2 tbsps chopped fresh mint leaves

1/2 tsp ground cardamom

1(2 inch) piece cinnamon stick

Directions

1. Okay let's begin this recipe by grabbing a frying pan or large skillet and mix in some veggie oil (two tbsps).

2. Once our veggie oil is hot add potatoes and fry them until they are a brownish color.

3. Once the potatoes are brown remove any excess oil and place them to the side for work later.

4. Keep the pan hot and add two more tbsps of oil and add some garlic, onion, and ginger.

5. Cook these contents until you find that your onions are nice and soft and slightly brown.

6. Now we want to add the following ingredients to our onions for seasoning: tomatoes, chili, salt, pepper, cumin, and turmeric.

Indo-Asian Chicken and Rice

7. Make sure that you vigorously stir the seasonings to protect them from burning while frying for about five mins.

8. Now we want to combine the following ingredients: a cinnamon stick, yogurt, cardamom, and mint.

9. Once these ingredients are added we want to place a lid over the pot and lower its heat to the lowest level.

10. Take care to stir the mixture every once and a while until you find that the tomatoes have been turned into a pulp.

11. You may notice that the mixture will become dry and sticky. If this is the case you will need to combine some hot water to the cooking pot occasionally.

12. Once the contents are thick. Grab your chicken pieces and combine them with the sauce.

13. You will want to make sure to mix the chicken well with the sauce so that every piece is evenly coated.

14. You now want to place a lid on the mixture and lower the temperature to its low level.

15. The chicken should be heated at this level while covered until you find that it is tender.

Typically this will take about 35 to 45 mins.

16. Cook the chicken down until you notice a bit of gravy left. If you find that the gravy is too much remove the lid from the cooking dish for a while and let the contents continue to cook.

17. Now let's get to the rice.

18. Get your rice and wash it until you find the water running clear. Drain the water with a colander and let the rice sit aside for about thirty mins.

19. Now grab a large frying pan or skillet and add some veggie oil with some onions and fry it up until it is nice and golden.

20. Grab the following ingredients and add them to the onions: rice, saffron, ginger, cardamom, cinnamon stick, and some cloves. Make sure that you stir consistently until you find that your rice is completely covered with spice.

21. Now we need to get another pot of a medium size.

22. Grab some chicken stock as well as some salt.

23. When you find that the rice is nice and hot you want to add this chicken stock and salt to it. Make sure that you combine everything well.

24. Now let's grab that chicken and potato pot from earlier.

25. We want to combine the chicken and potatoes nicely into the rice mixture.

26. Cover the rice pot with a lid and make sure it is completely sealed. We now want to take the temperature down to its lowest level and let this rice simmer for about 20 mins.

27. Make sure that you do not lift the lid while it is cooking.

28. After 20 mins has elapsed remove the lid and fluff the biryani.

29. It is now ready to be plated and served.

30. Enjoy.

23

How To Make Pilaf

Prep Time: 10 mins

Total Time: 50 mins

Servings per Recipe: 2

Calories 515

Fat 15.4

Carbohydrates 0

Protein 905

Cholesterol 87.1

Sodium 9.9

Ingredients

2 tbsp vegetable oil

3/4 tsp salt

1 onion, thinly sliced

1/2 tsp garam masala

1/2 tsp ground cumin

3/4 C. frozen mixed vegetables

1 C. Basmati rice, rinsed

2 C. water

Directions

1. Add oil in a pot over medium heat and cook until heated through.

2. Add the cumin and onion and stir fry for about 3-4 minutes.

3. Add the rice, vegetables, garam masala, salt and water and mix well.

4. Set the heat to high and cook until boiling.

5. Cover the pan and Set the heat to low.

6. Cook for about 10 minutes, without stirring.

7. Now, mix the rice mixture and cook for about 25-30 minutes.

8. Serve hot.

24

How to Make Pilaf

Rice Lunch Box

Prep Time: 15 mins

Total Time: 35 mins

(Raisin Salad)

Servings per Recipe: 4

Calories 451

Fat 13.7

Carbohydrates 41

Protein 218

Cholesterol 76.9

Sodium 8.3

Ingredients

1 1/2 C. brown rice

1/2 C. heavy cream

4 C. water

1 tsp curry powder

1 can asparagus tips, drained

1 tsp lemon juice

1 red bell pepper, seeded and diced

salt and pepper to taste

2 red apples, cored and diced

1/4 C. golden raisins

Directions

1. In a pot, add the water and rice and cook until boiling.

2. Set the heat to low and cook, covered for 25-30 minutes.

3. Drain any liquid from the rice and keep aside to cool completely.

4. Meanwhile, soak the raisins in water for about 20 minutes.

5. Drain the raisins completely.

6. In a bowl, add the cream and beat until soft peaks are formed.

7. Add the lemon juice, curry powder, salt and black pepper and gently, stir to combine.

8. In another bowl, add the raisins, apples, cooked rice, bell pepper and asparagus and mix.

9. Add the cream mixture and gently, stir to combine.

10. Refrigerate to chill completely before serving.

Rice Lunch Box

25

Rice Pudding

Prep Time: 5 mins

Total Time: 30 mins

Servings per Recipe: 4

Calories 423.4

Fat 27.0g

Cholesterol 46.8mg

Sodium 45.0mg

Carbohydrates 42.1g

Protein 7.0g

Ingredients

1 C. cooked long-grain rice

1/4 tsp ground cardamom

1 C. whole milk

1 1/2 oz. golden raisins

1/2 C. heavy cream

1 1/2 oz. chopped unsalted pistachios

3/4 C. coconut milk

2 oz. sugar

Directions

1. Add the whole milk and rice in a pan and cook over medium heat until boiling.

2. Set the heat to low and simmer for about 4-5 minutes, mixing as required.

3. Now, set the heat to medium and stir in the sugar, coconut milk, heavy cream and cardamom.

4. Cook for about 8-10 minutes, beating frequently.

5. Remove the pan from the heat.

6. immediately, add the pistachios and raisins and stir to combine.

7. In a serving bowl, place the pudding and with a plastic warp, cover the pudding surface.

8. Refrigerate to chill before serving.

26

Rice Pudding

20-Minute Rice Cooker

Prep Time: 5 mins

Total Time: 20 mins

Basmati

Servings per Recipe: 4

Calories 501.6

Fat 14.6g

Cholesterol

30.5mg

Sodium

769.3mg

Carbohydrates

81.6g

Protein 11.1g

Ingredients

2 C. basmati rice

2 C. frozen peas

4 C. water

cilantro

4 tbsp butter

1 tbsp turmeric

1 tsp salt

Directions

1. In the bowl of the rice cooker, add the rice, turmeric and salt and mixed until well combined.

2. Add the butter and water and set the rice cooker to cook.

3. Stir in the frozen peas and keep aside for a few minutes before serving.

4. Serve with a garnishing of the cilantro.

20-Minute Rice Cooker Basmati

27

Vermicelli Pilaf

Prep Time: 15 mins

Total Time: 45 mins

Servings per Recipe: 8

Calories 204.1

Fat 4.2g

Cholesterol

0.0mg

Sodium

150.6mg

Carbohydrates

37.6g

Protein 3.9g

Ingredients

5 tsp olive oil

1/2 tsp salt

3/4 C. chopped sweet onion

1/4 tsp black pepper

2 C. uncooked basmati rice

1/4 C. chopped parsley

3/4 C. uncooked vermicelli, broken into

1/4 C. chopped green onion

pieces

3 C. reduced-sodium fat-free chicken

broth

Directions

1. Set your oven to 350 degrees F before doing anything else.

2. In a Dutch oven, heat the oil over medium heat and cook the sweet onion for about 3

minutes, stirring frequently.

3. Stir in the vermicelli and rice and cook for about 2 minutes, stirring frequently.

4. Stir in the broth, salt and black pepper and bring to a boil.

5. Immediately, cover the pan and transfer into the oven.

6. Cook in the oven for about 15 minutes.

7. Remove from the oven and keep aide, covered for about 15 minutes.

8. Stir in the green onions and parsley and serve.

28

Vermicelli Pilaf

Peppery Pecan Basmati With Mushrooms

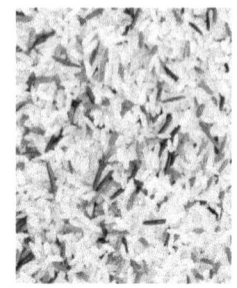

Prep Time: 10 mins

Total Time: 30 mins

Servings per Recipe: 6

Calories 176.4

Fat 5.9g

Cholesterol

0.2mg

Sodium

486.4mg

Carbohydrates

27.8g

Protein 3.9g

Ingredients

2 garlic cloves, minced

1/4 C. red pepper, chopped

2 tsp olive oil

1/4 tsp salt

1 C. basmati rice

1/8 tsp black pepper

2 tsp instant chicken bouillon granules

2 tbsp pecans, toasted and chopped

2 tsp lemon zest

6 lemon slices

4 oz. cremini mushrooms, sliced

4 green onions, sliced

Directions

1. In a medium pan, heat the oil and sauté the garlic for about 30 seconds.

2. Stir in the rice, bouillon granules and water and bring to a boil.

3. Reduce the heat to low and simmer, covered for about 10 minutes.

4. Stir in the mushrooms, red peppers, green onions, lemon zest, salt and pepper and simmer, covered for about 10 minutes.

5. Stir in the pecans and remove from the heat.

6. Serve with a garnishing of the lemon slices.

Peppery Pecan Basmati with Mushrooms

29

Milanese Basmati

Prep Time: 5 mins

Total Time: 30 mins

Servings per Recipe: 6

Calories 232.9

Fat 5.3g

Cholesterol

10.1mg

Sodium

617.6mg

Carbohydrates

42.0g

Protein 4.6g

Ingredients

1 1/2 C. basmati rice, rinsed

3 tbsp parsley, chopped

2 tbsp butter

2 tbsp dill, chopped

2 C. sweet onions, chopped

2 tbsp tarragon, chopped

2 1/2 C. water

1 1/2 tsp salt

Directions

1. In a large pan, melt the butter over medium-high heat and sauté the onions for about 5

minutes.

2. Stir in the rice, salt and water and bring to a boil.

3. Reduce the heat to low and simmer, covered for about 15 minutes.

4. Remove from the heat and keep aide, covered for about 10 minutes.

5. Season with the salt and black pepper and serve.

32

Milanese Basmati

Bashir's Basmati Pudding

Prep Time: 15 mins

Total Time: 3 hrs 15 mins

Servings per Recipe: 8

Calories 171.1

Fat 4.5g

Cholesterol

12.2mg

Sodium

50.1mg

Carbohydrates

27.5g

Protein 5.3g

Ingredients

4 C. whole milk

3/4 C. brown basmati rice, rinsed

1/3 C. demerara sugar

chopped unsalted pistachio nuts

2 tsp ground cardamom

Directions

1. Lightly grease a 3 1/2-quart slow cooker.

2. In a large pan, add the milk over medium heat and bring to a boil, stirring occasionally.

3. Stir in the cardamom and sugar and remove from the heat.

4. Stir in the rice and transfer the mixture into a prepared slow cooker.

5. Arrange a folded tea towel on top of the slow cooker pot.

6. Set the slow cooker on High and cook, covered for about 3 hours.

7. Uncover and transfer the pudding into a serving bowl. Keep aside at room temperature to cool.

8. Serve with a garnishing of the pistachios.

Bashir's Basmati Pudding

33

Turkey Basmati Bake

Prep Time: 5 mins

Total Time: 55 mins

Servings per Recipe: 6

Calories 614.5

Fat 38.8g

Cholesterol

166.7mg

Sodium

624.0mg

Carbohydrates

50.0g

Protein 18.2g

Ingredients

3 C. cooked white rice

salt

1 1/2 C. cooked wild rice

1/2 tsp ground black pepper

1 C. pecans, chopped and toasted

1/2 tsp Cajun spices

1/4 C. dried fruits, chopped e.g. apricots,

3 egg yolks, slightly beaten

cranberries and currants

2 C. roast turkey breast, shredded

6 tbsp butter

1 C. Gruyere cheese, grated

butter

1/4 C. cheddar cheese, grated

6 tbsp flour

3 C. milk

1 tsp salt

Directions

1. Set your oven to 350 degrees F before doing anything else and lightly, grease a 13x9-inch baking dish with some melted butter.

2. In a bowl, add the wild rice, basmati rice, dried fruit, pecans, salt and pepper and mix until well combined. For sauce: in a medium pan, melt 6 tbsp of the butter and add the flour, beating continuously. Cook for about 2 minutes, stirring continuously.

3. Slowly, add the milk, beating continuously.

4. Cook for about 4-6 minutes, stirring frequently.

5. Add the egg yolks, 1/2 tsp of Essence, salt and 1/2 tsp of pepper and beat until well combined. In the bottom of the prepared baking dish, place half of the rice mixture, followed by half of the turkey and half of the sauce. Repeat the layers and sprinkle with the both cheeses. Cook in the oven for about 40-45 minutes.

34

Turkey Basmati Bake

Easy Orzo Style

Prep Time: 5 mins

Total Time: 30 mins

Servings per Recipe: 5

Calories

192 kcal

Fat

5.1 g

Carbohydrates 31.7g

Protein

4.6 g

Cholesterol

12 mg

Sodium

265 mg

Ingredients

2 tbsps butter

1 cube chicken bouillon

1/2 C. uncooked orzo pasta

2 C. water

1/2 C. long-grain white rice

Directions

1. Fry your orzo in melted butter, in a saucepan, until toasted nicely. Then add in your bouillon, water, and rice.

2. Get the water boiling then lower the heat. Place a lid on the pan. Cook for 25 to 30 mins.

3. Enjoy warm.

Easy Orzo Style

35

Persian Pomegranate Rice Salad

Prep Time: 10 mins

Total Time: 25 mins

Servings per Recipe: 6

Calories 230.5

Fat 8.4g

Cholesterol

0.0mg

Sodium

393.9mg

Carbohydrates

36.3g

Protein 4.2g

Ingredients

2 C. water

pepper

1 C. basmati rice

3 seedless oranges

1 tsp salt

1/2 C. pomegranate seeds

1/4 C. white wine vinegar

1/4 C. toasted pine nuts

2 tsp grated orange rind

3 tbsp chopped parsley

1/4 C. orange juice

1 1/2 tbsp olive oil

Directions

1. In a pan, add the water and bring to a boil.

2. Add the rice and salt and stir to combine.

3. Reduce the heat to low and simmer, covered for about 15 minutes.

4. Remove from the heat and keep aide, covered for about 5 minutes.

5. With a fork, fluff the rice and keep aside to cool.

6. In a large serving bowl, add the cooked rice, pomegranate, oranges, parsley and pine nuts and mix.

7. In another bowl, add the orange rind, orange juice, vinegar, oil, salt and pepper and beat until well combined.

8. Pour the dressing over the rice salad and toss to coat well.

36

Persian Pomegranate Rice Salad

American Rice Chili

Prep Time: 15 mins

Total Time: 45 mins

Servings per Recipe: 4

Calories 472.4

Fat 4.9g

Cholesterol

49.9mg

Sodium

175.8mg

Carbohydrates

74.1g

Protein 33.7g

Ingredients

Chili

Toppings

vegetable oil cooking spray

3/4 small tomatoes

1 C. onion, chopped

1 1/4 green onions, sliced

3/4 tsp garlic, minced

1 tbsp green olives

3/4 tsp chopped ginger root

1 tsp green olives

1/2 jalapeño pepper, chopped

1 tbsp finely chopped cilantro

3 oz. mushrooms, chopped

1 tsp chopped cilantro

2 tsp flour

guacamole

11 oz. boneless skinless chicken breasts,

sour cream

cubed

salsa

1 1/4 lb. canned white beans, drained and corn tortilla strips rinsed

Rice

1 1/4 C. organic low sodium chicken broth

2 C. water

3/4 tsp dried oregano leaves

1 C. basmati rice

3/4 tsp ground cumin

1/8 tsp saffron

1/4 tsp ground coriander

1/8 tsp ground cinnamon

3/4 bay leaf

Directions

1. Grease a large pan with the cooking spray and heat over medium heat.

2. Add the onion, ginger, garlic and jalapeño and sauté for about 5 minutes.

3. Stir in the mushrooms and cook, covered for about 5 minutes.

4. Stir in the flour and cook for about 1 minute, stirring continuously.

5. Stir in the chicken, beans, herbs and chicken broth and bring to a boil.

6. Reduce the heat to low and simmer, covered for about 10-15 minutes.

American Rice Chili

37

7. Stir in salt and black pepper and remove from the heat.

8. Discard the bay leaf.

9. Meanwhile, for the rice: in a pan, add the water over high heat and bring to a boil.

10. Add the rice and saffron and stir to combine.

11. Reduce the heat to low and simmer, covered for about 15-20 minutes.

12. Remove from the heat and keep aide, covered for about 5 minutes.

13. With a fork, fluff the rice and serve.

14. Divide the chili into serving bowls and serve with a garnishing of the tomato, olives, green onion and cilantro alongside the rice, guacamole, sour cream, salsa and tortilla strips.

38

Cinnamon Sugar Basmati

Prep Time: 15 mins

Total Time: 40 mins

Servings per Recipe: 4

Calories 514.1

Fat 19.8g

Cholesterol

0.0mg

Sodium

589.5mg

Carbohydrates

76.5g

Protein 7.6g

Ingredients

2 C. basmati rice, soaked and rinsed

1 tsp cumin seed

1 medium onion, chopped

2 tsp brown sugar

6 cloves

5 tbsp sunflower oil

6 -8 green cardamoms, split

1 tsp marine salt

1 cinnamon stick

Directions

1. In a cast iron pan, heat the oil and sauté the onion for about 15 minutes, stirring frequently.

2. Stir in the cardamoms, cinnamon and cloves and cook until the cloves begin to swell.

3. Add the sugar and cook until sugar is caramelized, stirring continuously.

4. Sir in the cumin and cook for about 1 minute, stirring continuously.

5. Add the rice and stir to combine well.

6. Add enough boiling water to cover the rice by 1/3-inch.

7. Stir in the salt and increase the heat to high.

8. Cover the pan and cook for about 2 minutes.

9. Reduce the heat to medium and cook for about 3 minutes.

10. Reduce the heat to low and simmer, covered for about 10 minutes.

11. Remove from the heat and keep aide, covered for about 5 minutes.

12. Discard the whole spices and serve.

Cinnamon Sugar Basmati

39

Full Basmati Rice

Prep Time: 20 mins

Total Time: 1 hr 20 mins

Platter

Servings per Recipe: 8

Calories 279.2

Fat

0.0mg

Cholesterol

32.1mg

Sodium

36.1g

Carbohydrates 4.9g

Protein

Ingredients

1 1/2 C. basmati rice, rinsed

1/4 C. currants

kosher salt, if desired

silver aluminum foil

Toppings

Okra

1/2 C. dried onion flakes, toasted in a

1/4 lb. okra, trimmed and sliced

little oil

5 tbsp light vegetable oil

1/4 C. toasted slivered almonds, pan-

1 tsp lemon juice

toasted in a little ghee

1/4 C. toasted cashew nuts, pan-

toasted in a little ghee

Directions

1. In a large bowl of the water, soak the rice for about 30 minutes.

2. Meanwhile, for the okra: in a large frying pan, heat the oil over high heat.

3. Arrange the okra slices in a single layer and reduce the heat to medium.

4. Cook for about 20 minutes, flipping occasionally.

5. Stir in the lemon juice and remove from the heat.

6. With a slotted spoon, transfer the okra onto the paper towels-lined plate to drain.

7. Drain the rice well.

8. In a pan, add 12 C. of the water and salt and bring to a boil.

9. Stir in the rice and again bring to a boil.

10. Cook the rice for about 4 minutes.

11. Drain the rice well.

12. Transfer the rice into a greased 2-quart bowl and press to pack into the bowl.

13. Carefully, invert the rice onto a platter.

14. Serve with a decoration of onion flakes, crispy okra, currants and nuts.

Full Basmati Rice Platter

30-Minute Basmati Pilaf

Prep Time: 10 mins

Total Time: 30 mins

Servings per Recipe: 4

Calories 206.2

Fat 4.8g

Cholesterol

0.0mg

Sodium

586.6mg

Carbohydrates

36.7g

Protein 3.7g

Ingredients

1 tbsp canola oil

1 C. basmati rice

3 inches piece cinnamon sticks, halved

1 tsp table salt

2 green cardamom pods

1 1/2 C. water

2 whole cloves

1/4 C. sliced onion

Directions

1. In a medium pan, heat the oil and sauté the whole spices until they pop.

2. Add the onions and cook for about 2 minutes, stirring frequently.

3. Add the rice and cook for about 1 minute, stirring continuously.

4. Stir in the water and salt and bring to a boil.

5. Reduce the heat to low and simmer, covered for about 17 minutes.

6. Remove from the heat and keep aide, covered for about 10 minutes.

7. With a fork, fluff the rice and serve.

30-Minute Basmati Pilaf

43

Ginger Basmati With Eggplant

Prep Time: 10 mins

Total Time: 40 mins

Servings per Recipe: 4

Calories 555.7

Fat 20.1g

Cholesterol

41.6mg

Sodium

1857.0mg

Carbohydrates

84.4g

Protein 14.7g

Ingredients

Directions

Veggies

1. For the Vegetables: in a large soup

1/4 C. ghee

pan, melt the ghee over medium-

1/2 C. onion, chopped

high heat and cook the onions, ginger,

3 garlic cloves, chopped

garlic, jalapeño, cumin seeds and

1 tsp cumin seed

mustard seeds until the onions are

1/2 tsp mustard seeds

translucent.

1 tbsp ginger, grated

2. Stir in the eggplant and cook for

1 fresh jalapeño pepper

about 8 minutes, stirring occasionally.

1 eggplant, cubed

Add the spinach and cook, covered

1 bunch spinach, rinsed

for a few minutes.

4 tomatoes, chopped

3. Stir in the tomatoes, turmeric and salt

1 tsp turmeric

and cook for about 10 minutes.

1 1/2 tsp salt

4. Add the garbanzo beans, sugar and

15 oz. garbanzo beans

lemon juice and cook for about 5

1 tbsp lemon juice, fresh

minutes.

1 tbsp sugar

5. Meanwhile, for the spiced rice: in a

Rice

pan, add the water and bring to a

1 C. white basmati rice, rinsed

rolling boil.

2 C. water

6. Add the rice, ghee, and spices and mix

1 tsp salt

well.

1 tsp turmeric

1 tbsp ginger , grated

7. Reduce the heat to low and simmer,

1 tbsp ghee

covered for about 25-30 minutes.

8. Remove from the heat and keep aide,

covered for about 5 minutes. With a

fork, fluff the rice and serve alongside

the stew.

44

Ginger Basmati with Eggplant

Azza's Basmati Salad

Prep Time: 20 mins

Total Time: 40 mins

Servings per Recipe: 6

Calories 279.8

Fat 14.3g

Cholesterol

0.0mg

Sodium

304.7mg

Carbohydrates

34.6g

Protein 4.7g

Ingredients

Salad

1 tbsp walnut oil

1 1/4 C. uncooked brown basmati rice,

1 1/2 tbsp sherry wine vinegar

rinsed

2 tsp ginger, grated

1/2 tsp salt

1 -2 tsp liquid honey

2 -3 stalks celery, chopped

1/4 tsp salt

100 g dried cranberries

1/4 tsp pepper

1/2 C. walnuts, chopped

Dressing

2 tbsp peanut oil

Directions

1. In a pan, add the rice, salt and required amount of the boiling water and cook according to the package's directions.

2. In a sieve, rinse the cooked rice with running cold water.

3. Drain completely and transfer into a bowl.

4. Add the cranberries, celery and walnuts and mix.

5. For the vinaigrette: in a bowl, add all the ingredients and beat until well combined.

6. Pour the vinaigrette over the rice salad and gently, toss to coat.

Azza's Basmati Salad

45

Karachi Style Rice And Chicken Salad

Prep Time: 40 mins

Total Time: 1 hr 5 mins

Servings per Recipe: 6

Calories 390.9

Fat 11.1g

Cholesterol

39.6mg

Sodium

650.0mg

Carbohydrates

51.2g

Protein 23.0g

Ingredients

Salad

1 (14 oz.) cans artichoke hearts, drained

1 1/2 C. water

and chopped

1 C. uncooked basmati rice

Dressing

3 garlic cloves, minced

1/4 C. fat-free chicken broth

2 C. shredded rotisserie cooked boneless

3 tbsp lemon juice

skinless chicken breasts

3 tbsp extra virgin olive oil

1/2 C. sliced green onion

1 tsp Dijon mustard

1/4 C. chopped drained sun-dried

3/4 tsp salt

tomato

1/2 tsp ground black pepper

1 tsp grated lemon rind

1/4 tsp dried oregano

1 (15 1/2 oz.) cans chickpeas, rinsed

and drained

Directions

1. For the salad: in a 3-quart pan, add the water and bring to a boil.

2. Add the rice and garlic and stir to combine. Reduce the heat to low and simmer, covered for about 20 minutes. Remove from the heat and keep aide, covered for about 5 minutes.

3. Transfer the rice into a large bowl. Add the chicken, green onion, sun-dried tomato, lemon rind, chickpeas and artichoke hearts and gently, stir to combine. For the dressing: in a bowl, add all ingredients and beat until well combined.

4. Pour the dressing over the rice salad and gently, toss to coat.

46

Karachi Style Rice and Chicken Salad

Basmati Kerala

Prep Time: 5 mins

Total Time: 50 mins

Servings per Recipe: 4

Calories 182.9

Fat 1.4g

Cholesterol

0.0mg

Sodium

16.3mg

Carbohydrates

38.3g

Protein 4.0g

Ingredients

1 C. brown basmati rice, rinsed and

1/4 C. diced red bell pepper

drained

1 tsp season salt

2 C. water

1/2 tsp dried jalapeño pepper

1 tbsp dried onion flakes

1/2 tsp cumin

1/4 C. julienne carrot

1/4 C. diced celery

Directions

1. In a medium pan, add the water over high heat and bring to a boil.

2. Add the rice and remaining ingredients and cook according to package's directions.

Basmati Kerala

47

Ginger Garlic Basmati With Squash

Prep Time: 10 mins

Total Time: 30 mins

Servings per Recipe: 8

Calories 247.5

Fat 9.0g

Cholesterol

20.3mg

Sodium 390.9mg

Carbohydrates

39.0g

Protein 4.2g

Ingredients

1 lb. butternut squash, peeled, seeded

1 1/2 C. basmati rice, rinsed and drained

and cut into cubes

1 1/2 tbsp curry powder

2 C. minced onions

1/2 tsp salt

3 tbsp minced ginger

3 C. de-fatted chicken broth

1 tbsp minced garlic

2 tbsp chopped cilantro

1/3 C. butter

Directions

1. In a 5-6-quart pan, melt the butter over medium heat and cook onions, garlic and ginger for about 10-15 minutes, stirring frequently.

2. Add the rice and cook for about 5 minutes, stirring occasionally.

3. Add the curry powder and cook for about 30 seconds, stirring continuously.

4. Stir in the squash, broth and 1/2 tsp of the salt and bring to a boil over high heat.

5. Reduce the heat to low and simmer, covered for about 16-18 minutes, stirring occasionally.

6. Stir in the cilantro and salt and serve.

48

Ginger Garlic Basmati with Squash

60-Minute Basmati

Prep Time: 40 mins

Total Time: 55 mins

Servings per Recipe: 6

Calories 265.7

Fat 6.3g

Cholesterol

0.0mg

Sodium

5.6mg

Carbohydrates

47.1g

Protein 4.9g

Ingredients

350 g basmati rice, rinsed

Onions

2 cloves

2 tbsp vegetable oil

1 inch cinnamon stick

1 onion, sliced

2 bay leaves

2 tbsp chopped coriander

3 green cardamom pods

1 1/2 tsp cumin seeds

Directions

1. In a large bowl of the water, soak the rice for about 30 minutes.

2. Drain the rice well.

3. In a pan, add a liter of water and bring to a boil.

4. Add the rice and whole spices and boil for about 5-8 minutes.

5. Drain the rice and keep aside, covered.

6. In a frying pan, heat the oil and fry the onion for about 5-10 minutes or until crispy.

7. Transfer the onion onto a paper towel-lined plate to drain.

8. Serve the rice with a topping of the crispy onions and coriander.

60-Minute Basmati

49

Creamy Pineapple Rice

Prep Time: 15 mins

Total Time: 35 mins

Servings per Recipe: 4

Calories

470 kcal

Fat

33.2 g

Carbohydrates 42.3g

Protein

3.2 g

Cholesterol

122 mg

Sodium

35 mg

Ingredients

1/3 C. white rice

1 C. crushed pineapple, drained

1 1/2 C. heavy cream

1/3 C. white sugar

Directions

1. Get a large pot. Add to the pot some water and your rice. Bring everything to a rolling boil.

Then lower a heat. Place a lid on the pot and let your rice cook for 22 mins. Make sure your rice is tender, then remove excess liquids (but there should not be any).

2. Put the rice in the fridge. Get a bowl, mix until light and fluffy: sugar and cream.

3. Finally take your rice out of the fridge add in your cream and sugar and also your pineapple.

4. Enjoy in bowls, chilled or at room temp.

52

Creamy Pineapple Rice

Nutty Rice

Prep Time: 5 mins

Total Time: 45 mins

Servings per Recipe: 4

Calories

280 kcal

Fat

16.1 g

Carbohydrates 31g

Protein

4.3 g

Cholesterol

0 mg

Sodium

210 mg

Ingredients

1 C. brown rice

1/4 tsp ground ginger

2 tbsps margarine

1/4 tsp ground black pepper

1/4 C. finely diced onion

1/4 tsp salt

1/2 C. finely diced pecans

2 tbsps minced parsley

1/4 tsp dried basil

Directions

1. Get a large pot and add your rice to it. Also add about two C. or water. Bring everything to a rolling boil. Then set the heat to low. Place a lid on the pot and cook the rice for 42

mins. Turn off the heat when the rice is tender.

2. Simultaneously while the rice is cooking fry the following in margarine: salt, onions, pepper, pecans, ginger, basil, and parsley.

3. Stir fry this mix until the onions are soft.

4. Add your seasoned onions and pecans to your brown rice and mix evenly.

5. Enjoy warm.

Nutty Rice

53

Middle Eastern Style Rice

Prep Time: 5 mins

Total Time: 40 mins

Servings per Recipe: 6

Calories

377 kcal

Fat

17.1 g

Carbohydrates 29.5g

Protein

26.6 g

Cholesterol

74 mg

Sodium

584 mg

Ingredients

1 1/2 lb lean ground beef

1 tsp beef bouillon granules

3 tbsps garlic powder

1/4 C. pine nuts

2 tbsps ground cinnamon

1 squeeze lemon juice, or to taste

1 tbsp ground allspice

4 C. water

2 C. long-grain rice

Directions

1. Get a frying pan and fry your beef with allspice, garlic powder, and cinnamon, until fully cooked for 12 mins. Crumble the beef after it is done.

2. Add the following to your beef, and mix it nicely: beef bouillon, rice, and water. Bring the mixture to a boiling state, then lower the heat and let the rice lightly simmer for 22 mins.

3. Simultaneously while the rice is cooking toast your pine nuts with no oil for 5 mins.

4. Garnish your rice with some lemon juice and the pine nuts.

5. Enjoy immediately.

54

Middle Eastern Style Rice

Rice Casserole

Prep Time: 20 mins

Total Time: 45 mins

Servings per Recipe: 8

Calories

461 kcal

Fat

20.3 g

Carbohydrates 35.3g

Protein

32 g

Cholesterol

118 mg

Sodium

975 mg

Ingredients

1 lb ground beef

2 1/4 C. shredded mozzarella cheese

1 (26 oz.) jar spaghetti sauce

2 C. cottage cheese

1/2 tsp garlic powder

3 C. cooked rice, cooled

2 eggs, lightly beaten

3/4 C. shredded Parmesan cheese, divided

Directions

1. Set your oven to 375 degrees before doing anything else.

2. Fry your beef for 8 mins and remove any excess oil then crumble it. Add in your garlic powder, and evenly mix everything then add in your tomato sauce, and mix one more time.

3. Get a bowl, and combine: eggs, rice, and one fourth a C. of parmesan.

4. Get a 2nd bowl, combine: one fourth C. parmesan, cottage cheese, and two C. of mozzarella.

5. Get a casserole dish and coat it with nonstick spray, then layer the following: half of your rice, half of your cheese, half of your beef and tomato sauce.

6. Continue until the casserole dish is full or all the ingredients are used.

7. Cook in the oven for 27 mins. Let the casserole cool.

8. Enjoy.

Rice Casserole

55

White Rice And Tomatoes

Prep Time: 20 mins

Total Time: 1 hr 10 mins

Servings per Recipe: 5

Calories

422 kcal

Fat

2.8 g

Carbohydrates 92g

Protein

10.7 g

Cholesterol

2 mg

Sodium

1120 mg

Ingredients

1 slice turkey bacon, diced

1 pinch red pepper flakes

1/2 onion, diced

2 (14 oz.) cans whole kernel corn, drained

1/4 green bell pepper, diced

3 1/2 C. water

1/2 tsp diced fresh thyme

2 C. white rice

1/2 C. tomato sauce

1 tsp browning sauce

1 tsp salt

1/2 tsp ground black pepper

Directions

1. Fry your bacon. Then remove any excess oils.

2. Combine with the bacon: thyme, onions, and bell peppers.

3. Stir fry until the onions are see-through. Lower the heat under the pan and add in: pepper flakes, tomato sauce, black pepper, salt, and browning sauce.

4. Cook the sauces for 4 mins. Then combine in your water and stir everything. Increase the heat to get the water and sauces boiling. Once boiling add in your rice, then stir it, then lower the heat again.

5. Place a lid on the pan and cook the rice for 32 mins.

6. Stir your rice after it is done and enjoy warm.

56

White Rice and Tomatoes

Jalapeno And Cream Rice

Prep Time: 15 mins

Total Time: 1 hr

Servings per Recipe: 6

Calories

207 kcal

Fat

12.1 g

Carbohydrates 17.9g

Protein

7.8 g

Cholesterol

30 mg

Sodium

830 mg

Ingredients

1/3 C. uncooked long grain white rice

2 tbsps butter

2/3 C. water

1/2 C. diced onion

1 (10.75 oz.) can condensed cream of

1 (10 oz.) package frozen diced spinach,

chicken soup, undiluted

thawed and drained

1/4 C. milk

4 oz. processed cheese food, cubed

2 fresh jalapeno peppers, seeded and diced

1/2 tsp salt

1/4 tsp ground black pepper

Directions

1. Get a casserole dish and coat it with nonstick spray or oil and set your oven to 375

degrees before doing anything else.

2. Get a saucepan and add in your water and rice. Bring the water to a rolling boil and then set the heat to low and place a lid on the pot. Cook the rice for 22 mins.

3. Get a bowl and evenly mix: pepper, soup, salt, jalapenos, and milk.

4. Fry your onions in melted butter until soft. Then add in your spinach. Cook for 1 more min. Then combine in your cooked rice.

5. Finally add in your soup and heat everything up. Add the cheese and then dump everything into your greased casserole dish.

6. Cook the casserole in the oven for 27 mins. Let the contents cool.

7. Enjoy.

Jalapeno and Cream Rice

57

Easy Meaty Rice

Prep Time: 5 mins

Total Time: 45 mins

Servings per Recipe: 4

Calories

361 kcal

Fat

14 g

Carbohydrates 35.5g

Protein

23.8 g

Cholesterol

69 mg

Sodium

814 mg

Ingredients

1 lb ground beef

2 C. water

1 (6.9 oz.) package chicken flavored rice

mix

Directions

1. Fry your beef until fully done and then crumble it and remove any excess oils. This should take about 8 mins.

2. Add your rice to the beef and toast it for 6 mins.

3. Combine in the water and packet seasonings and place a lid on the skillet.

4. Get all the contents boiling and then set the heat to low and cook the rice for 30 mins.

5. Enjoy.

58

Easy Meaty Rice

Maggie's Favorite Rice

Prep Time: 10 mins

Total Time: 40 mins

Servings per Recipe: 8

Calories

465 kcal

Fat

33.7 g

Carbohydrates 21.1g

Protein

19.7 g

Cholesterol

89 mg

Sodium

747 mg

Ingredients

1 tbsp butter, or as needed

2 (4 oz.) cans diced green chilies

3 C. cooked rice, or more to taste

1/2 C. grated Cheddar cheese

2 C. sour cream

salt to taste

1 lb shredded Monterey Jack cheese

Directions

1. Coat a baking dish with butter and set your oven to 350 degrees before doing anything else.

2. Add to the baking dish the following (in order): rice, salt, sour cream, green chilies, and Monterey. Top with some cheddar.

3. Cook for 32 mins in the oven. Let the contents cool.

4. Enjoy.

Maggie's Favorite Rice

59

Beef And Onion Rice

Prep Time: 15 mins

Total Time: 55 mins

Servings per Recipe: 6

Calories

269 kcal

Fat

10 g

Carbohydrates 35.9g

Protein

8.5 g

Cholesterol

20 mg

Sodium

792 mg

Ingredients

1/4 C. butter

3/4 C. diced carrots

1 1/4 C. long-grain rice

3/4 C. diced celery

2 (10.5 oz.) cans beef consommé

1/4 C. sliced almonds

1/2 tsp salt

3/4 C. diced green onions

Directions

1. Set your oven to 375 degrees before doing anything else.

2. For 5 mins fry your rice in melted butter until toasted and browned. Add some salt and your consommé over the rice and get everything boiling. Once boiling enter the contents into a baking dish.

3. Cook the rice in the oven for 30 mins. Then add in come almonds, green onions, celery, and carrots to the rice and stir it nicely. Place it back in the oven for 5 more mins.

4. Enjoy.

62

Beef and Onion Rice

Parsley Butter Rice

Prep Time: 15 mins

Total Time: 50 mins

Servings per Recipe: 6

Calories

131 kcal

Fat

2.4 g

Carbohydrates 24.7g

Protein

2.4 g

Cholesterol

5 mg

Sodium

23 mg

Ingredients

1 tbsp butter

1/2 tsp dried parsley

1 C. diced onion

1 bay leaf

1 clove garlic, minced

1 C. minced green bell pepper

3 1/3 C. water

1 1/2 C. converted rice

Directions

1. Fry your onions for 5 mins in melted butter until see-through, in a saucepan.

2. Add the garlic into the onions and cook for another 3 mins.

3. Add in bell peppers and cook for 2 more mins.

4. Finally combine with the peppers and onions: water, bay leaf, parsley and rice.

5. Bring everything to a rolling boil and once boiling place a lid on the pot, set the heat to low, and then cook the rice for 22 mins until soft.

6. Let the contents cool for a bit.

7. Enjoy.

Parsley Butter Rice

63

Latin Style Rice

Prep Time: 15 mins

Total Time: 35 mins

Servings per Recipe: 6

Calories

203 kcal

Fat

6.3 g

Carbohydrates 31.4g

Protein

4.1 g

Cholesterol

15 mg

Sodium

607 mg

Ingredients

3 tbsps butter

2 tsps chili powder

1 C. diced onions

2 tsps beef bouillon granules

1 C. diced green bell pepper

1/2 tsp salt

1/2 C. diced celery

3 C. cooked white rice

1 clove garlic, minced

1 (28 oz.) can minced tomatoes with

juice

Directions

1. Stir fry the following in butter: garlic, onions, celery, and green bell peppers for 12 mins.

2. Add in your rice, salt, tomatoes with juice, beef bouillon, and chili powder.

3. Heat until lightly boiling and let the contents simmer for 22 mins until the rice is tender.

4. Enjoy.

64

Latin Style Rice

Easy Persian Style Rice

Prep Time: 10 mins

Total Time: 1 hr 20 mins

Servings per Recipe: 5

Calories

404 kcal

Fat

10.2 g

Carbohydrates 69.5g

Protein

7.1 g

Cholesterol

24 mg

Sodium

812 mg

Ingredients

2 C. uncooked long-grain rice

1 onion, chopped

3/4 tsp crushed saffron threads

3 C. boiling vegetable broth

4 tbsps butter

1 tsp salt

6 whole cardamom seeds

4 whole cloves

3 cinnamon sticks

Directions

1. Soak your rice in a bowl covered in cold water for 32 mins.

2. Get a 2nd bowl, and soak your saffron in 2 tbsps of boiling water.

3. Stir fry your cinnamon, cardamom, and cloves for 3 mins, then combine in onions and fry until they are browned. Once the onions are browned add in your rice and let it simmer for 7 mins.

4. Add in your broth at this point and let it boil.

5. Then add in your saffron water and some salt. Place a lid on the pan and set the heat to low and let the rice cook for 40 mins.

Easy Persian Style Rice

65

Bacon, Apples, And Mushroom

Prep Time: 15 mins

Total Time: 45 mins

White Rice

Servings per Recipe: 12

Calories

209 kcal

Fat

7 g

Carbohydrates 28.6g

Protein

8.4 g

Cholesterol

14 mg

Sodium

388 mg

Ingredients

3 C. water

1 Granny Smith apple - peeled, cored and

1 1/2 C. uncooked white rice

diced

3 slices turkey bacon

1 C. cooked, chopped turkey meat

1/2 onion, chopped

1 tsp chicken soup base

2 stalks celery, diced

3 tbsps soy sauce

1 carrot, chopped

1/2 C. chopped parsley

1/2 C. peas

ground black pepper to taste

1 C. fresh mushrooms, sliced

1/2 C. slivered almonds

1/2 C. raisins

Directions

1. Get a large pot and get some water boiling in it. Then mix in your rice.

2. Once boiling set the heat to low, place a lid on the pot and let the rice cook for 20 mins.

3. Fry your bacon until crispy and remove any excess oils.

4. Then add in your apple, onions, raisins, celery, almonds, mushrooms, peas, and carrots.

5. Continually stir over a lower heat until tender.

6. Finally add in the following: pepper, rice, turkey, parsley, chicken soup base, and soy sauce.

7. Mix everything evenly.

8. Enjoy.

66

Bacon, Apples, and Mushroom White Rice

Basmati Peas And Peanut Rice

Prep Time: 10 mins

Total Time: 30 mins

Servings per Recipe: 4

Calories

302 kcal

Fat

9.5 g

Carbohydrates 45.7g

Protein

9 g

Cholesterol

0 mg

Sodium

318 mg

Ingredients

1 C. uncooked basmati rice

1/2 C. frozen petite peas, thawed

2 1/4 C. water

1/2 C. dry roasted peanuts

1/2 tsp salt

1/4 tsp ground turmeric

Directions

1. Bring the following to a rolling boil: turmeric, rice, salt, and water. Once boiling set the heat to low, place a lid on the pot, and let the rice cook for 22 mins.

2. After the cooking time has elapsed add in your peanuts and then your peas. Mix everything nicely.

3. Then serve once the peas have been warmed.

Basmati Peas and Peanut Rice

67

Longhorn Beef And Cheddar Rice

Prep Time: 30 mins

Total Time: 1 hr

Servings per Recipe: 10

Calories

391 kcal

Fat

17.4 g

Carbohydrates 33.9g

Protein

22 g

Cholesterol

69 mg

Sodium

771 mg

Ingredients

3 C. water

1 (28 oz.) can peeled and diced tomatoes

2 C. uncooked long grain white rice

1 1/2 tsps salt

6 slices turkey bacon

1/4 tsp ground black pepper

1 1/2 lb ground beef

1 1/2 C. shredded Cheddar cheese

1 onion, chopped

1/2 green bell pepper, seeded and

chopped

Directions

1. Set your oven to 400 degrees before doing anything else.

2. Bring the following to a rolling boil: water and rice.

3. Set the heat to low and then place a lid on the pot and let the rice cook for 22 mins until tender. Fry your bacon simultaneously until crispy. Set aside 2 tbsps of oil. Then crumble the bacon.

4. Once the bacon is crumbled remove it from the pan and add in: onions, ground beef, and green peppers. Cook everything until the beef is fully done. Then remove all excess oils and add some pepper and salt for taste. Now grab a casserole dish and put the rice and beef mix into it. Then add bacon, beef mix, bacon oil, and tomatoes.

5. Combine everything nicely. Then garnish the dish with some cheddar. Cook in the oven for 35 mins.

6. Enjoy.

68

Longhorn Beef and Cheddar Rice

West African Style Rice

Prep Time: 20 mins

Total Time: 1 hr 20 mins

Servings per Recipe: 8

Calories

332 kcal

Fat

13.4 g

Carbohydrates 33.5g

Protein

19.8 g

Cholesterol

46 mg

Sodium

713 mg

Ingredients

1 tbsp olive oil

2 C. water

1 large onion, sliced

1 (3 lbs) whole chicken, cut into 8 pieces

2 (14.5 oz.) cans stewed tomatoes

1 C. uncooked white rice

1/2 (6 oz.) can tomato paste

1 C. diced carrots

1 tsp salt

1/2 pound fresh green beans, trimmed and

1/4 tsp black pepper

snapped into 1 to 2 inch pieces

1/4 tsp cayenne pepper

1/4 tsp ground nutmeg

1/2 tsp red pepper flakes

1 tbsp Worcestershire sauce

1 tsp chopped fresh rosemary

Directions

1. Fry your onions in oil until they are see-through. Then add in tomato paste and tomato sauce, rosemary, salt, cayenne, red pepper flakes, and Worchestshire.

2. Bring everything to a rolling boil, then set the heat low, put in the water and the chicken pieces, and place a lid on the pot. Let the chicken simmer for 35 mins.

3. After 35 mins of simmering add in green beans, nutmeg, rice and carrots.

4. Get everything boiling again with high heat and then lower the heat.

5. Place a lid back on the pot and let the rice cook for 27 mins until soft.

6. Enjoy.

West African Style Rice

69

Chili And Cilantro Jasmine

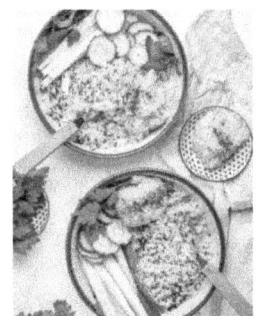

Prep Time: 15 mins

Total Time: 30 mins

Servings per Recipe: 4

Calories

634 kcal

Fat

17.3 g

Carbohydrates 84.4g

Protein

32.8 g

Cholesterol

68 mg

Sodium

562 mg

Ingredients

4 tbsps vegetable oil

1 tbsp fish sauce

5 cloves garlic, finely chopped

1 tbsp soy sauce

2 green chilies, diced

2 tsps chopped green onion

2 C. cubed skinless, boneless chicken

2 tbsps chopped fresh basil leaves

breast meat

5 tbsps chopped fresh cilantro

2 C. cooked jasmine rice, chilled

1 tbsp white sugar

Directions

1. Fry your garlic in a wok in oil and then add your chicken, and chili peppers. Stir fry until the chicken is fully cooked.

2. Once the chicken is cooked add in: soy sauce, sugar, rice, and fish sauce. Stir fry for 2 mins then add in your cilantro, green onions, and basil cook for another 2 mins. Then enjoy.

72

Chili and Cilantro Jasmine

Herbs And Onion Potatoes

Prep Time: 15 mins

Total Time: 2 hrs 20 mins

Servings per Recipe: 6

Calories

356 kcal

Fat

9.9 g

Carbohydrates 60.4g

Protein

8.2 g

Cholesterol

18 mg

Sodium

410 mg

Ingredients

5 large potatoes, peeled and thinly sliced

3/4 tsp salt

3/4 C. chopped onion

1/4 tsp dried parsley

3 tbsps butter

1/4 tsp poultry seasoning

1/4 C. all-purpose flour

1/8 tsp ground black pepper

1 3/4 C. low-sodium chicken broth

1/4 C. chopped fresh chives

2 tbsps mayonnaise

2 cloves garlic, minced

Directions

1. Get a casserole dish and coat it with nonstick spray or grease it with oil. Then set your oven to 325 degrees before doing anything else.

2. Get a pan and mix butter and flour together until completely smooth and even with a medium heat level. Then combine in: pepper, broth, poultry seasoning, mayo, parsley, garlic and salt. Stir for two mins. Get your casserole dish and layer your potatoes and then your onions. Cover your onions with the heated wet mix of mayo. Place some foil around the casserole dish and bake for 1 hr and 50 mins. Then cook for another 10 mins with no covering.

3. Garnish with some chives before serving.

Herbs and Onion Potatoes

73

Basic Baked Potato

Prep Time: 3 mins

Total Time: 1 hr 33 mins

Servings per Recipe: 1

Calories

128 kcal

Fat

0.1 g

Carbohydrates 29.7g

Protein

2.7 g

Cholesterol

0 mg

Sodium

7 mg

Ingredients

1 potato

Directions

1. Set your oven to 350 degrees for doing anything else.

2. Clean your potato. Then get a fork and poke some holes throughout it.

3. Simply bake the potato in the oven for 1 hr and 45 mins 74

Basic Baked Potato

Better Baked Potato

Prep Time: 15 mins

Total Time: 1 hr 30 mins

Servings per Recipe: 8

Calories

422 kcal

Fat

29.5 g

Carbohydrates 29.3g

Protein

10.9 g

Cholesterol

63 mg

Sodium

537 mg

Ingredients

4 large baking potatoes

1/2 tsp pepper

8 slices turkey bacon

1 C. shredded Cheddar cheese, divided

1 C. sour cream

8 green onions, sliced, divided

1/2 C. milk

4 tbsps butter

1/2 tsp salt

Directions

1. Set your oven to 350 degrees before doing anything else.

2. Cook the potatoes for 1 hour in the hot oven.

3. While the potatoes are baking fry your bacon in a pan.

4. Then once the bacon is crispy, remove all extra oil, and break it into pieces and place it to the side.

5. After the potatoes are finished let them sit for 12 mins. Then cut the potatoes into two pieces.

6. Scoop out all of the insides of the potato and put it in a bowl. Combine it with half of your green onions, sour cream, half of your cheese, milk, pepper, and salt.

7. Combine everything until completely smooth and even then fill each skin with some mix.

8. Garnish the mix with bacon, green onions, and cheese.

9. Cook in the oven for another 15 to 20 mins.

10. Enjoy.

Better Baked Potato

75

Cheddar And Bacon Potato Soup

Prep Time: 15 mins

Total Time: 40 mins

Servings per Recipe: 6

Calories

748 kcal

Fat

49.3 g

Carbohydrates 49.7g

Protein

27.2 g

Cholesterol

85 mg

Sodium

1335 mg

Ingredients

12 slices turkey bacon

1 1/4 C. shredded Cheddar cheese

2/3 C. margarine

1 C. sour cream

2/3 C. all-purpose flour

1 tsp salt

7 C. milk

1 tsp ground black pepper

4 large baked potatoes, peeled and

cubed

4 green onions, chopped

Directions

1. Fry your bacon. Then remove excess oils. Then break the bacon into pieces for later.

2. Melt down your margarine in a Dutch oven. Then add in flour and mix it nicely.

3. Continue stirring and pouring in milk. Keep stirring until everything is thick.

4. Then add onion and potatoes.

5. Get everything boiling. Once boiling, set the heat to low and let it simmer for 12 mins.

6. Combine in your bacon, pepper, cheese, salt, and sour cream. And let the contents simmer for 5 more mins.

7. Enjoy.

76

Cheddar and Bacon Potato Soup

Cheesy Bacon Baked

Prep Time: 25 mins

Total Time: 1 hr 45 mins

Potato Salad

Servings per Recipe: 8

Calories

421 kcal

Fat

29.4 g

Carbohydrates 26.7g

Protein

13.8 g

Cholesterol

49 mg

Sodium

844 mg

Ingredients

8 medium potatoes, sliced

1 C. mayonnaise

1/2 lb sliced turkey bacon

salt and pepper to taste

1 lb processed American cheese, sliced

1/4 C. black olives, sliced

1/2 onion, chopped

Directions

1. Coat a casserole dish with butter. Then set your oven to 325 degrees before doing anything else.

2. Get a saucepan and enter into it, your potato slices and put enough water to cover the potatoes.

3. Let the contents boil for 10 mins. The remove all the water and put it to the side.

4. Fry your bacon. Then remove excess oils.

5. Get a bowl, mix evenly: pepper, potatoes, salt, cheese, mayo, and onions.

6. Put contents into a casserole dish and garnish with olives and bacon.

7. Cook in the oven for 1 hr.

8. Enjoy.

Cheesy Bacon Baked Potato Salad

77

Ultimate Baked Potato

Prep Time: 15 mins

Total Time: 1 hr 30 mins

Servings per Recipe: 4

Calories

859 kcal

Fat

50.3 g

Carbohydrates 73.5g

Protein

31.3 g

Cholesterol

135 mg

Sodium

1497 mg

Ingredients

4 large baking potatoes

1 tsp salt

1/2 lb turkey bacon

1 (8 oz.) container sour cream

4 tbsps butter

1 (8 oz.) package shredded Cheddar

1 large onion, chopped

cheese

1/2 C. chopped fresh mushrooms

1 tsp dry bread crumbs

1 tsp crushed red pepper

1 tsp garlic powder

1 tsp ground black pepper

1 tsp chopped fresh chives

Directions

1. Set your oven to 400 degrees before doing anything else.

2. Get your potatoes and poke holes into them with a fork.

3. Cook in the oven for 1 hr. Fry your bacon in the meantime. Once crispy remove excess oils and break them into pieces.

4. Fry your mushrooms, chives, onion, salt, red pepper, black pepper, and garlic in butter until onions are tender.

5. Once the potatoes are done. Cut them in half and remove all the flesh from the skin and put it in a bowl.

6. Combine in sour cream, half of the cheese, and onion mix with the potato insides. Refill the skins with the mix.

7. Then garnish with any bacon and cheese that is remaining.

8. Cook in the oven for another 20 mins. Enjoy.

78

Ultimate Baked Potato

Mashed Potatoes Done Correctly

Prep Time: 20 mins

Total Time: 1 hr 35 mins

Servings per Recipe: 12

Calories

295 kcal

Fat

14.9 g

Carbohydrates 35.6g

Protein

6.2 g

Cholesterol

57 mg

Sodium

129 mg

Ingredients

5 lb Yukon Gold potatoes, peeled and

1 onion, grated

cubed

1 egg

1/2 C. butter

salt and pepper to taste

1/4 C. milk

1 (8 oz.) package cream cheese, softened

Directions

1. Set your oven to 350 degrees before doing anything else.

2. Boil potatoes in salt and water for 17 mins. Remove all water.

3. Then put the potatoes in a bowl and mash them while combining in milk and butter.

4. Then add in onions, and sour cream.

5. Get a 2nd bowl, mix: eggs and a small amount of mashed potatoes.

6. Combine both bowls. Add in pepper and salt. Put everything in a baking container and cook in the oven for 1 hr.

Mashed Potatoes Done Correctly

79

Cheddar And Onion Potato

Prep Time: 20 mins

Total Time: 1 hr 50 mins

Soup

Servings per Recipe: 6

Calories

686 kcal

Fat

46.3 g

Carbohydrates 45.4g

Protein

23.4 g

Cholesterol

128 mg

Sodium

988 mg

Ingredients

4 baking potatoes

1/2 tsp ground black pepper

2/3 C. butter

12 slices cooked turkey bacon, crumbled

2/3 C. all-purpose flour

5 oz. shredded Cheddar cheese

6 C. milk

1 (8 oz.) container sour cream

1 C. chopped green onions

3/4 tsp salt

Directions

1. Set your oven to 400 degrees before doing anything else.

2. Cook the potatoes in the oven for 1 hr. Then remove them from the oven and remove the flesh of each potato after cutting it in half. Set everything aside. Throw away the skins.

3. Form a roux with some melted butter and flour this should take 1 min of stirring. (Melt butter first, then add in flour and keep stirring).

4. Add in your milk and keep stirring until everything becomes thick.

5. Once your mix is thick combine in: cheese, potatoes, bacon, green onions, black pepper, and salt.

6. Cook everything with a medium level of heat for about 17 mins. Add sour cream before the cooking time has elapsed.

7. Enjoy.

82

Cheddar and Onion Potato Soup

Sweet Potato Casserole

Prep Time: 15 mins

Total Time: 40 mins

Servings per Recipe: 12

Calories

433 kcal

Fat

20.5 g

Carbohydrates 60.3g

Protein

4.1 g

Cholesterol

65 mg

Sodium

170 mg

Ingredients

2 (29 oz.) cans sweet potatoes in light

1 C. brown sugar

syrup, drained

1/2 C. all-purpose flour

1/2 C. white sugar

1 C. pecan halves

1/2 C. butter, melted

2 eggs, beaten

1 tsp vanilla extract

1/3 C. milk

1/3 C. butter, melted

Directions

1. Set your oven to 350 degrees before doing anything else.

2. Put your potatoes in a bowl and mash them up nicely.

3. Then add in milk, sugar, vanilla, half a C. of melted butter, and eggs. Continue mixing until everything is nicely even.

4. Get a 2nd bowl, mix evenly: flour, 1/3 melted butter, pecans, and brown sugar.

5. Get a casserole dish and fill it with your mashed potatoes and then top the potatoes with your pecan mixture.

6. Cook in the oven for 27 mins.

7. Enjoy.

Sweet Potato Casserole

83

Potatoes And Garlic

Prep Time: 5 mins

Total Time: 1 hr 5mins

Servings per Recipe: 4

Calories

225 kcal

Fat

6.9 g

Carbohydrates 37.5g

Protein

4.4 g

Cholesterol

0 mg

Sodium

919 mg

Ingredients

4 medium baking potatoes, scrubbed

salt and pepper to taste

2 tbsps olive oil

2 tsps garlic salt, or to taste

Directions

1. Set your oven to 375 degrees before doing anything else.

2. Get a smaller bowl: add in olive oil.

3. Get a 2nd smaller bowl add in: pepper, and garlic salt.

4. Cover your potatoes with olive oil, by dipping, or rolling them in the bowl of oil. Then coat them with the dry seasonings.

5. Cook the potatoes for 1 hr in the oven directly on the rack.

6. Enjoy.

84

Potatoes and Garlic

Sweet Potatoes Ii

Prep Time: 20 mins

Total Time: 1 hr 5 mins

Servings per Recipe: 7

Calories

449 kcal

Fat

21.7 g

Carbohydrates 61g

Protein

5.4 g

Cholesterol

84 mg

Sodium

315 mg

Ingredients

3 1/2 C. mashed sweet potatoes

1/2 tsp ground nutmeg

1/4 C. milk

1/2 tsp ground cinnamon

1/4 C. orange juice

1/4 C. butter, softened

2 eggs, beaten

3/4 C. packed light brown sugar

1 tsp vanilla extract

1/2 C. all-purpose flour

1/2 C. white sugar

3/4 C. chopped pecans

1/2 tsp salt

3 tbsps butter, softened

Directions

1. Coat a casserole dish with oil or nonstick spray. Then set your oven to 350 degrees before doing anything else.

2. Get a bowl, mix: cinnamon, potatoes, nutmeg, milk, butter, eggs, salt, vanilla, and sugar.

3. Enter this into your casserole dish.

4. Get a 2nd bowl, evenly mix: pecans, one fourth C. of butter, flour, and brown sugar.

5. Top your sweet potatoes with this mix.

6. Cook everything in the oven for 50 mins.

7. Enjoy.

Sweet Potatoes II

85

Baked Potatoes Remix

Prep Time: 10 mins

Total Time: 1 hr 15 mins

Servings per Recipe: 4

Calories

321 kcal

Fat

7.3 g

Carbohydrates 61g

Protein

4.8 g

Cholesterol

0 mg

Sodium

92 mg

Ingredients

2 tbsps olive oil

2 pinches salt

3 large sweet potatoes

2 pinches ground black pepper

2 pinches dried oregano

Directions

1. Coat a casserole dish with olive oil. Then set your oven to 350 before doing anything else.

2. Clean and remove the skin from your potatoes.

3. Cut them into bit sized chunks.

4. Enter the potatoes in the casserole dish and stir them so they get coated with olive oil.

5. Season the potatoes with pepper, oregano, and salt.

6. Cook in the oven for 1 hr.

7. Enjoy.

86

Baked Potatoes Remix

Dip For Baked Potatoes

Prep Time: 10 mins

Total Time: 8 hrs 10 mins

Servings per Recipe: 16

Calories

125 kcal

Fat

11 g

Carbohydrates 2.2g

Protein

4.8 g

Cholesterol

32 mg

Sodium

326 mg

Ingredients

1 (8 oz.) package cream cheese, softened

1 C. shredded Cheddar cheese

1 (8 oz.) container sour cream

2/3 (3 oz.) can real bacon bits

1 (1 oz.) package ranch dressing mix

3 green onions, thinly sliced

Directions

1. Get a bowl, evenly mix: cheddar, ranch dressing mix, bacon bits, sour cream, green onions, and cream cheese.

2. Chill in the fridge for 8 hours.

3. Enjoy with some fried potatoes or any baked potato recipe.

Dip for Baked Potatoes

87

Pecan And Sweet Potato Casserole

Prep Time: 15 mins

Total Time: 55 mins

Servings per Recipe: 6

Calories

570 kcal

Fat

40.8 g

Carbohydrates 47.9g

Protein

6.6 g

Cholesterol

131 mg

Sodium

262 mg

Ingredients

2 sweet potatoes, peeled and cubed

1 tsp vanilla extract

1 C. brown sugar

1/3 C. butter, melted

1/2 C. butter

1 C. chopped pecans

1/2 C. milk

1/3 C. all-purpose flour

2 large eggs

Directions

1. Coat a baking dish with nonstick spray or oil. Then set your oven to 375 degrees before doing anything else.

2. Boil the potatoes in water and salt for 23 mins. Remove all liquid and mash the potatoes.

3. Get a bowl and put in 3 C. of potatoes and the following: vanilla extract, brown sugar, eggs, half a C. of butter, and milk.

4. Mix with an electric mixer or by hand until very smooth.

5. Put everything your baking dish.

6. Get a 2nd bowl, mix: pecans, one third C. of melted butter, and flour.

7. Mix until smooth.

8. Then pour over the sweet potatoes in the baking dish.

9. Cook in the oven for 27 mins.

10. Enjoy.

88

Pecan and Sweet Potato Casserole

Part 2

Simple Grilled Cauliflower

"This is a perfect side dish to any meal coming off the bbq. Simple, quick, and tasty!"

Serving: 4 | Prep: 10 m | Cook: 10 m | Ready in: 20 m

Ingredients

- 1 head cauliflower, cut into large florets
- 3 tablespoons olive oil
- 1 teaspoon coarse sea salt
- 1 teaspoon cracked black pepper

Direction

- Preheat grill for medium heat and lightly oil the grate.
- Place cauliflower in a bowl. Drizzle olive oil over cauliflower and season with salt and pepper; toss to evenly coat.
- Cook on the preheated grill, turning every 2 minutes, until cauliflower is golden brown, 10 to 15 minutes.

Nutrition Information

- Calories: 127 calories
- Total Fat: 10.3 g
- Cholesterol: 0 mg
- Sodium: 484 mg
- Total Carbohydrate: 8 g
- Protein: 2.9 g

Simple Roasted Butternut Squash

"Butternut squash is so good on its own, that barely any seasoning is needed. This recipe is so simple and easy."

Serving: 4 | Prep: 15 m | Cook: 25 m | Ready in: 40 m

Ingredients

- 1 butternut squash - peeled, seeded, and cut into 1-inch cubes
- 2 tablespoons olive oil
- 2 cloves garlic, minced
- salt and ground black pepper to taste

Direction

- Preheat oven to 400 degrees F (200 degrees C).
- Toss butternut squash with olive oil and garlic in a large bowl. Season with salt and black pepper. Arrange coated squash on a baking sheet.
- Roast in the preheated oven until squash is tender and lightly browned, 25 to 30 minutes.

Nutrition Information

- Calories: 177 calories
- Total Fat: 7 g
- Cholesterol: 0 mg
- Sodium: 11 mg
- Total Carbohydrate: 30.3 g
- Protein: 2.6 g

Simple Roasted Squash Mash

"A simple way to make roasted squash that tastes delicious with roasts of any kind or great on its own."
Serving: 4 | Prep: 5 m | Cook: 45 m | Ready in: 50 m
Ingredients

- 2 tablespoons olive oil
- 2 tablespoons slivered almonds
- 3 zucchini, cut into short strips
- salt and freshly ground black pepper to taste

Direction

- Preheat the oven to 400 degrees F (200 degrees C).
- Place squash in the preheated oven and bake until easily pierced with a knife, 45 to 60 minutes.
- Cut baked squash in half lengthwise, remove seeds with a spoon. Remove meat from skin and place into a serving bowl. Mash squash with butter, brown sugar, cinnamon, and salt.

Nutrition Information

- Calories: 258 calories
- Total Fat: 11.8 g
- Cholesterol: 31 mg
- Sodium: 386 mg
- Total Carbohydrate: 40.8 g
- Protein: 2.7 g

Simple Steamed Artichokes

"These steamed artichokes are delicious and light, perfect for an appetizer. Dip the leaves in melted butter or mayonnaise."

Serving: 2 | Prep: 10 m | Cook: 20 m | Ready in: 30 m

Ingredients

- 2 whole artichokes
- 1 clove garlic
- 1 tablespoon lemon juice
- 1 bay leaf

Direction

- Cut stem from artichokes and discard, making sure the bottom of each artichoke is flat. Cut top 1 inch (or so) of the artichoke and discard. Snip the thorny ends from each artichoke leaf with a pair of kitchen scissors.
- Fill the bottom of a pot with a couple of inches of water, adding garlic, lemon juice, and bay leaf to the water. Place a steamer basket in the pot, making sure that the water does not flow over the bottom of the steamer basket.
- Place the artichokes in the basket, resting on the flattened bottoms.
- Bring water to a boil, cover the pot, and cook until the leaves can be easily pulled from the artichoke, 20 to 30 minutes.

Nutrition Information

- Calories: 65 calories
- Total Fat: 0.2 g
- Cholesterol: 0 mg

- Sodium: 121 mg
- Total Carbohydrate: 14.7 g
- Protein: 4.3 g

Simply Sesame Asparagus

"Perfect for grilling! A simple and easy dish to prepare that's packed with great flavor. I love to serve this in the summer with grilled meats or salmon."
Serving: 4 | Prep: 10 m | Cook: 10 m | Ready in: 20 m
Ingredients

- 1 pound fresh asparagus, trimmed
- 1/4 cup sesame oil
- 1 tablespoon coarse salt

Direction

- Preheat an outdoor grill for medium-high heat and lightly oil the grate.
- Toss asparagus and sesame oil together in a bowl until asparagus is completely coated. Season with coarse salt.
- Cook asparagus on the preheated grill, turning every 2 minutes, until browned and tender yet still crisp to the bite, about 8 minutes.

Nutrition Information

- Calories: 143 calories
- Total Fat: 13.8 g
- Cholesterol: 0 mg
- Sodium: 1442 mg

- Total Carbohydrate: 4.4 g
- Protein: 2.5 g

Skillet Apples With Cinnamon

"Easy fried apples make a great side dish for breakfast or dinner."
Serving: 6 | Prep: 10 m | Cook: 10 m | Ready in: 20 m
Ingredients

- 1/4 cup butter
- 8 apples, cored and chopped
- 1/2 cup brown sugar
- 1/4 teaspoon ground cinnamon
- 1/4 teaspoon nutmeg

Direction

- Melt butter in a large, heavy skillet over medium heat. Sauté apples, brown sugar, cinnamon, and nutmeg in hot butter until tender and golden, 10 to 15 minutes.

Nutrition Information

- Calories: 234 calories
- Total Fat: 8 g
- Cholesterol: 20 mg
- Sodium: 61 mg
- Total Carbohydrate: 43.5 g
- Protein: 0.6 g

Skillet Summer Squash

"The good old-fashioned country way. This is definitely NOT diet food. You don't drain the bacon fat off after you brown it. If you really have to, you can substitute butter, but it won't be the same. You can also use this recipe with a combination of yellow and pattypan squash."

Serving: 4 | Prep: 15 m | Cook: 35 m | Ready in: 50 m

Ingredients

- 4 slices bacon, cut into small pieces
- 1 onion, chopped
- 2 pounds summer squash, sliced diagonally 1/2 inch thick
- salt and ground black pepper to taste

Direction

- Cook and stir bacon in a skillet over medium heat until crisp, 8 to 10 minutes. Add onions and cook in the bacon drippings until softened, 3 to 5 minutes. Add squash, salt, and black pepper; stir to coat.
- Cover skillet and cook squash mixture over low heat until tender, about 25 minutes.

Nutrition Information

- Calories: 182 calories
- Total Fat: 13.2 g
- Cholesterol: 19 mg
- Sodium: 239 mg
- Total Carbohydrate: 11.9 g
- Protein: 5.7 g

Skinny Mashed Potatoes

"A very good and tasty alternative to mashed potatoes made without all the butter and cream! Garnish with chopped parsley or chives and a little bit of butter, if desired."

Serving: 6 | Prep: 20 m | Cook: 20 m | Ready in: 40 m

Ingredients

- 8 potatoes, peeled and diced
- 2 large onions, cut into chunks
- 2 cloves garlic, minced, or more to taste
- 1 cube vegetable bouillon, or more to taste
- water

Direction

- Place potatoes, onions, garlic, and bouillon cube in a large pot. Pour in enough water to cover contents half-way; bring to a boil. Reduce heat to medium-low and simmer until potatoes are tender, about 15 minutes.
- Mash potatoes in the cooking liquid to desired smoothness.

Nutrition Information

- Calories: 229 calories
- Total Fat: 0.3 g
- Cholesterol: 0 mg
- Sodium: 22 mg
- Total Carbohydrate: 52.1 g
- Protein: 6.1 g

Slow Cooker Cider Applesauce No Sugar Added

"This spicy applesauce requires no added sugar because the apples and spices are sweet enough on their own. The smell of the apples cooking with the spices makes the entire house smell like apple cider!"

Serving: 16 | Prep: 10 m | Cook: 4 h | Ready in: 4 h 10 m

Ingredients

- 5 pounds apples - peeled, cored, and thinly sliced
- 1 1/2 tablespoons ground cinnamon
- 1/2 teaspoon ground cloves
- 1/4 teaspoon ground nutmeg

Direction

- Layer apples into a slow cooker. Sprinkle cinnamon, cloves, and nutmeg over the apples.
- Cook on High until apples are soft, 4 to 5 hours. Whisk apples vigorously for a chunkier-style applesauce. Puree with an immersion blender for a smoother applesauce.

Nutrition Information

- Calories: 76 calories
- Total Fat: 0.3 g
- Cholesterol: 0 mg
- Sodium: 2 mg
- Total Carbohydrate: 20.2 g
- Protein: 0.4 g

Smashed Cauliflower Side Dish

"Wonderfully creative substitute for potatoes or rice. Surprise your family with this excellent side dish!"

Serving: 4 | Prep: 10 m | Cook: 10 m | Ready in: 20 m

Ingredients

- 2 (16 ounce) packages frozen cauliflower
- 1/4 cup butter
- 1/4 teaspoon ground black pepper
- 1/2 teaspoon salt
- 1 clove garlic, minced (optional)

Direction

- Place cauliflower in a pot with enough water to cover. Bring to a boil and cook 10 minutes, or until tender. Drain and return cauliflower to pot.
- Stir butter, black pepper, salt, and garlic into cooked cauliflower.
- Mash cauliflower mixture with a potato masher or whisk until a smooth consistency similar to mashed potatoes.

Nutrition Information

- Calories: 158 calories
- Total Fat: 12.1 g
- Cholesterol: 31 mg
- Sodium: 427 mg
- Total Carbohydrate: 11 g
- Protein: 4.7 g

Smoky Golden Mashed Potatoes

"Smoky Golden Mashed Potatoes is a wonderful recipe to have on hand for any occasion. Just add bacon and gouda cheese to our Buttery Golden Selects Flavored Mashed Potatoes for a delicious side dish that is easy and quick!"

Serving: 4 | Prep: 5 m | Ready in: 5 m

Ingredients

- 1 (4 ounce) package Idahoan® Buttery Golden Selects Mashed Potatoes
- 1 (3 ounce) package bacon bits*
- 1/2 cup Gouda cheese, shredded

Direction

- Follow package direction and prepare mashed potatoes.
- Stir in bacon and cheese and serve.

Nutrition Information

- Calories: 128 calories
- Total Fat: 8.6 g
- Cholesterol: 32 mg
- Sodium: 783 mg
- Total Carbohydrate: 0.3 g
- Protein: 12.7 g

Sous Vide Cauliflower

"With so many great Asian dishes (check out Chef John's carmel chicken for example) on this site we are always looking for interesting side dishes to pair with them. This simply invented sous vide side proved to be a a great accompaniment. My family fights over who gets to finish it."

Serving: 4 | Prep: 10 m | Cook: 40 m | Ready in: 50 m

Ingredients

- 1 head cauliflower, cut into 2-inch chunks
- 1 teaspoon soy sauce
- 1 teaspoon fish sauce
- 1/4 teaspoon cayenne pepper
- ground black pepper to taste

Direction

- Preheat water in sous vide vessel to 185 degrees F (85 degrees C).
- Combine cauliflower, soy sauce, fish sauce, cayenne pepper, and black pepper in a bowl and toss to coat. Place mixture into sous vide bag and vacuum-seal.
- Cook cauliflower mixture in sous vide water bath until tender, about 40 minutes.

Nutrition Information

- Calories: 38 calories
- Total Fat: 0.2 g
- Cholesterol: 0 mg
- Sodium: 209 mg

- Total Carbohydrate: 8 g
- Protein: 3 g

Southern Fried Apples

"I have a very basic recipe to add some sweetness to breakfast or any meal. Serve garnished with additional cinnamon if desired."

Serving: 4 | Prep: 10 m | Cook: 10 m | Ready in: 20 m

Ingredients

- 1/2 cup butter
- 1/2 cup white sugar
- 2 tablespoons ground cinnamon
- 4 Granny Smith apples - peeled, cored, and sliced

Direction

- Melt butter in a large skillet over medium heat; stir sugar and cinnamon into the hot butter. Add apples and cook until apples begin to break down, 5 to 8 minutes.

Nutrition Information

- Calories: 369 calories
- Total Fat: 23.1 g
- Cholesterol: 61 mg
- Sodium: 165 mg
- Total Carbohydrate: 44.9 g
- Protein: 0.8 g

Southern Fried Cabbage With Bacon Mushrooms And Onions

"Fattening? Oh yeah. Worth it? Oh yeah!"
Serving: 10 | Prep: 15 m | Cook: 30 m | Ready in: 45 m
Ingredients

- 1 pound bacon
- 1 large head cabbage, chopped
- 1 large onion, chopped
- 1 (8 ounce) package sliced fresh mushrooms
- salt and ground black pepper to taste

Direction

- Place bacon in a large skillet and cook over medium-high heat, turning occasionally, until evenly browned, about 10 minutes. Drain the bacon slices on paper towels; crumble when cooled. Drain all but 3 tablespoons of bacon drippings from skillet.
- Cook and stir cabbage, onion, and mushrooms in the remaining bacon drippings until tender and lightly browned, about 20 minutes. Fold bacon into cabbage mixture. Season with salt and black pepper.

Nutrition Information

- Calories: 123 calories
- Total Fat: 6.4 g
- Cholesterol: 16 mg
- Sodium: 368 mg
- Total Carbohydrate: 9.6 g

- Protein: 8 g

Spaghetti Cacio E Pepe

"This is a recipe that we have made in our family for many years--everyone loves it. It's a very basic and easy variation on mac 'n cheese."

Serving: 4 | Prep: 5 m | Cook: 18 m | Ready in: 23 m

Ingredients

- 1 pound spaghetti
- 6 tablespoons olive oil
- 2 cloves garlic, minced
- 2 teaspoons ground black pepper
- 1 3/4 cups grated Pecorino Romano cheese

Direction

- Bring a large pot of lightly salted water to a boil. Cook spaghetti in the boiling water, stirring occasionally until tender yet firm to the bite, about 10 minutes. Scoop out some of the cooking water and reserve. Drain spaghetti.
- Heat oil in a large skillet over medium heat. Add garlic and pepper; cook and stir until fragrant, 1 to 2 minutes. Add spaghetti and Pecorino Romano cheese. Ladle in 1/2 cup of reserved cooking water; stir until cheese is melted, about 1 minute. Add more cooking water until sauce coats spaghetti, about 1 minute more.

Nutrition Information

- Calories: 806 calories

- Total Fat: 36 g
- Cholesterol: 54 mg
- Sodium: 633 mg
- Total Carbohydrate: 87.8 g
- Protein: 31.6 g

Spargel In Schinken White Asparagus Wrapped In Ham

"A very simple yet delicious way to wrap freshly cooked white asparagus in ham slices. You need as many ham slices as asparagus spears. This dish is traditionally served with new potatoes."

Serving: 4 | Prep: 15 m | Cook: 20 m | Ready in: 35 m

Ingredients

- 2 1/4 pounds white asparagus
- salt to taste
- 1/4 cup butter, divided
- 1 pinch white sugar
- 7 ounces sliced ham

Direction

- Peel asparagus spears from top to bottom with a vegetable peeler, starting below the tips. Cut off woody ends with a knife.
- Place asparagus spears in a large, wide saucepan and pour in enough lightly salted water to just cover. Bring water to a boil; add 1 tablespoon butter and sugar. Reduce heat;

simmer until spears are tender and easily pierced with a knife, 15 to 25 minutes. Drain well.

- Melt remaining 3 tablespoons butter in a small pot over low heat.
- Wrap each asparagus spear with a slice of ham. Arrange on a serving plate; drizzle melted butter on top.

Nutrition Information

- Calories: 274 calories
- Total Fat: 20.9 g
- Cholesterol: 58 mg
- Sodium: 755 mg
- Total Carbohydrate: 10.2 g
- Protein: 14.8 g

Spicy Sweet Potatoes

"The sweetness of the potatoes is offset by the spiciness of the Cajun pepper. Adjust the pepper to taste. My family absolutely loves this recipe!"

Serving: 4 | Prep: 15 m | Cook: 1 h | Ready in: 1 h 15 m

Ingredients

- 4 sweet potatoes, peeled and cubed
- 6 tablespoons olive oil
- 2 tablespoons brown sugar
- 1 teaspoon Cajun pepper seasoning
- 1 pinch kosher salt

Direction

- Preheat oven to 375 degrees F (190 degrees C).
- Place sweet potatoes, olive oil, brown sugar, Cajun seasoning, and salt in a large resealable plastic bag; shake to coat potatoes evenly. Transfer mixture to a baking dish.
- Bake in preheated oven, stirring occasionally, until sweet potatoes are tender, about 1 hour.

Nutrition Information

- Calories: 402 calories
- Total Fat: 20.4 g
- Cholesterol: 0 mg
- Sodium: 346 mg
- Total Carbohydrate: 52.6 g
- Protein: 3.6 g

Spiralized Brown Butter Sage Sweet Potato

"Fabulous and simplistic dish for those who don't like 'sweet' sweet potatoes. You can easily substitute butternut squash in this dish. Makes 3 large helpings or 4 medium-sized helpings."
Serving: 4 | Prep: 10 m | Cook: 9 m | Ready in: 19 m

Ingredients

- 1 large sweet potato, peeled and halved crosswise
- 1 tablespoon olive oil, or more as needed
- 1/4 cup butter
- 9 fresh sage leaves
- salt to taste

Direction

- Cut sweet potato into spaghetti-like ribbons with a spiralizer.
- Heat olive oil in a large nonstick skillet over medium heat. Add sweet potato ribbons; cook, stirring often and adding more oil to prevent sticking, until starting to soften, 6 to 7 minutes. Transfer to a plate.
- Heat butter in the same skillet until melted and foaming, about 1 minute. Add sage leaves; swirl until butter is a rich caramel color and leaves are crisp and dark green, 2 to 3 minutes. Remove sage leaves from the butter. Add sweet potato; stir to coat well.
- Season sweet potato with salt and garnish with crisp sage leaves.

Nutrition Information

- Calories: 231 calories
- Total Fat: 15 g
- Cholesterol: 31 mg
- Sodium: 183 mg
- Total Carbohydrate: 23 g
- Protein: 1.9 g

Steamed Broccoli

"A quick and simple broccoli recipe. Skip the bacon, swap olive oil for butter, toss in some cheese; whatever you like."
Serving: 2 | Prep: 10 m | Cook: 5 m | Ready in: 15 m
Ingredients

- 1 head broccoli, cut into florets
- 1 slice cooked bacon, chopped

- 1 tablespoon butter
- salt and ground black pepper to taste

Direction

- Place a steamer insert into a saucepan and fill with water to just below the bottom of the steamer. Bring water to a boil. Add broccoli, cover, and steam until tender, 3 to 5 minutes.
- Mix steamed broccoli, bacon, butter, salt, and pepper together in a bowl.

Nutrition Information

- Calories: 118 calories
- Total Fat: 7.6 g
- Cholesterol: 19 mg
- Sodium: 160 mg
- Total Carbohydrate: 10 g
- Protein: 5.4 g

Steamed Broccoli And Carrots With Lemon

"This side dish adds lots of color and vitamins and minerals to your meal."

Serving: 2 | Prep: 10 m | Cook: 5 m | Ready in: 15 m

Ingredients

- 1 cup broccoli florets
- 1/2 cup julienne-cut carrots
- 2 tablespoons lemon juice
- 1 teaspoon seasoned salt, or to taste

Direction

- Place a steamer insert into a saucepan and fill with water to just below the bottom of the steamer. Bring water to a boil. Add broccoli florets and carrots, cover, and steam until tender, about 5 minutes.
- Transfer vegetables to a bowl; add lemon juice and seasoned salt and toss to coat.

Nutrition Information

- Calories: 35 calories
- Total Fat: 0.3 g
- Cholesterol: 0 mg
- Sodium: 497 mg
- Total Carbohydrate: 8.1 g
- Protein: 1.7 g

Steamed Mashed Cauliflower

"Steamed head of cauliflower without butter, milk, extra calories, or carbs. Very light, very tasty. My 12-year-old child is very picky, but absolutely loves my faux mashed potatoes as they are very similar in texture and taste to the real thing. As an extra we've even added roasted garlic cloves. Heavenly!"

Serving: 4 | Prep: 10 m | Cook: 5 m | Ready in: 15 m

Ingredients

- 1 head cauliflower, cut into florets
- 1 (4 ounce) log herbed goat cheese (chevre)
- cracked black pepper to taste

Direction

- Place cauliflower florets in a large microwave-safe bowl with enough water to just cover the bottom of the bowl.
- Cover bowl loosely with waxed paper or a paper towel and steam cauliflower in microwave on high until tender, 4 to 5 minutes; drain.
- Place drained cauliflower in a food processor with goat cheese and puree until completely smooth; season with black pepper.

Nutrition Information

- Calories: 140 calories
- Total Fat: 8.6 g
- Cholesterol: 22 mg
- Sodium: 189 mg
- Total Carbohydrate: 8.5 g
- Protein: 9 g

Steamy Microwave Zucchini

"Super easy, healthy vegetables with great flavor!"
Serving: 4 | Prep: 15 m | Cook: 6 m | Ready in: 23 m

Ingredients

- 2 zucchini, sliced
- 2 stalks celery, chopped
- 1 small onion, chopped
- 4 large fresh mushrooms, sliced
- 1/2 cup shredded Cheddar cheese

Direction

- Mix zucchini, celery, onion, and mushrooms in a microwave-safe dish. Cover dish with plastic wrap.
- Cook on High until vegetables are steamed and slightly tender, about 6 minutes.
- Pull plastic wrap away from dish, stir vegetables, sprinkle Cheddar cheese over the vegetables, and replace the plastic to seal tightly. Let dish sit until the cheese melts, 2 to 3 minutes. Stir vegetables to coat evenly with melted cheese.

Nutrition Information

- Calories: 82 calories
- Total Fat: 4.9 g
- Cholesterol: 15 mg
- Sodium: 111 mg
- Total Carbohydrate: 5.1 g
- Protein: 5.3 g

Stir Fried Sugar Snap Peas

"Living in China, I had to adapt to some foods I hadn't eaten before. Sugar snap peas have become one of my favorites, and while trying new concoctions, I came up with this delicious and easy recipe! Easy, green, and tasty - three of my favorite things!"
Serving: 4 | Prep: 10 m | Cook: 8 m | Ready in: 18 m

Ingredients

- 2 cups sugar snap peas, strings removed
- 2 tablespoons olive oil
- 2 cloves garlic, minced

- 2 tablespoons soy sauce

Direction

- Place a steamer insert into a saucepan and fill with water to just below the bottom of the steamer. Bring water to a boil. Add snap peas, cover, and steam until tender, about 2 minutes.
- Heat oil in a non-stick skillet over medium-high heat; sauté garlic until nearly brown, about 2 minutes. Pour in snap peas and soy sauce. Cook and stir until snap peas begin to brown, about 4 minutes.

Nutrition Information

- Calories: 110 calories
- Total Fat: 6.8 g
- Cholesterol: 0 mg
- Sodium: 451 mg
- Total Carbohydrate: 8.7 g
- Protein: 2.8 g

Sugar Pumpkin Puree

"Making pumpkin puree is easy and fun. The kids love it, you can make so many varieties of recipes with this puree. The seeds can be roasted as well. Store in the freezer in freezer-safe bags or can and preserve."

Serving: 8 | Prep: 15 m | Cook: 1 h | Ready in: 1 h 15 m

Ingredients

- 1 sugar pumpkin - cut into eighths, seeded, and pulp removed

Direction

- Preheat oven to 325 degrees F (165 degrees C). Arrange pumpkin pieces on a baking sheet.
- Bake in the preheated oven until pumpkin meat is tender, about 1 hour.
- Scrape pumpkin meat from the peel and transfer meat to a blender; blend until smooth.

Nutrition Information

- Calories: 52 calories
- Total Fat: 0.2 g
- Cholesterol: 0 mg
- Sodium: 2 mg
- Total Carbohydrate: 12.9 g
- Protein: 2 g

Super Duper Applesauce Grandmas Secret Revealed

"For years my grandma made this sauce. It is amazingly delicious, do try it."
Serving: 4 | Prep: 5 m | Cook: 30 m | Ready in: 8 h 35 m

Ingredients

- 3 apples, cored and chopped
- 2 teaspoons lemon juice
- 2 teaspoons honey

Direction

- Place 1 apple in a bowl. Cover with water. Let soak until soft, 8 hours to overnight. Drain, reserving soaking water.
- Transfer soaked apple to a large pot. Mix in lemon juice and honey. Simmer over low heat, stirring occasionally, until consistency is very soft, about 15 minutes. Add remaining 2 apples to the pot. Continue simmering, adding some of the soaking water, until applesauce reaches desired consistency, 15 to 45 minutes.

Nutrition Information

- Calories: 66 calories
- Total Fat: 0.2 g
- Cholesterol: 0 mg
- Sodium: 1 mg
- Total Carbohydrate: 17.6 g
- Protein: 0.3 g

Sweet And Spicy Sweet Potato Baked Fries

"This recipe came after visiting a restaurant and trying to duplicate it at home! It is easy, too. Serve with honey mustard."

Serving: 2 | Prep: 10 m | Cook: 30 m | Ready in: 40 m

Ingredients

- 2 tablespoons olive oil
- 1 tablespoon honey
- 1 teaspoon cayenne pepper
- 1/2 teaspoon cracked black pepper

- 1 sweet potato, cut into long thin slices, or more as needed

Direction

- Preheat oven to 400 degrees F (200 degrees C).
- Mix olive oil, honey, cayenne pepper, and black pepper in a large bowl. Add sweet potato slices; toss to coat. Arrange coated sweet potatoes on a baking sheet.
- Bake in the preheated oven until fries are slightly crisp, 30 to 40 minutes.

Nutrition Information

- Calories: 278 calories
- Total Fat: 13.7 g
- Cholesterol: 0 mg
- Sodium: 79 mg
- Total Carbohydrate: 38.1 g
- Protein: 2.4 g

Sweet And Yummy Mashed Acorn Squash

"If you're having trouble trying to find something to do with the acorn squash in your refrigerator, this sweet side is perfect for kids and for adults too! If you would like some more cinnamon or brown sugar, feel free to add some more."

Serving: 4 | Prep: 10 m | Cook: 1 h | Ready in: 1 h 10 m

Ingredients

- 2 acorn squash, halved and seeded
- 1 pinch ground cinnamon
- 1/4 cup butter

- 2 teaspoons salt
- 1 pinch brown sugar

Direction

- Preheat oven to 400 degrees F (200 degrees C). Place acorn squash, cut-side down, on a baking sheet.
- Bake in the preheated oven for 30 minutes. Flip squash and sprinkle cinnamon into the center and dot with butter. Continue baking until flesh can be easily pierced with a fork, about 30 minutes more.
- Scoop flesh into a bowl and mix in brown sugar until evenly combined.

Nutrition Information

- Calories: 203 calories
- Total Fat: 11.8 g
- Cholesterol: 31 mg
- Sodium: 1252 mg
- Total Carbohydrate: 26.5 g
- Protein: 2.1 g

Sweet Corn On The Cob Without The Cob

"I always seem to want sweet corn when it's not in season, and sometimes the canned sweet corn has a funky flavor. Now you can have quick sweet corn all year round! Using real salted butter makes a huge difference in this case. Tastes just like in-season corn on the cob."

Serving: 3 | Prep: 5 m | Cook: 5 m | Ready in: 10 m

Ingredients

- 1 (15.25 ounce) can whole kernel corn, drained
- 1 teaspoon white sugar
- 1 tablespoon salted butter
- salt and ground black pepper to taste

Direction

- Stir corn, butter, and sugar together in a saucepan over low heat; cook and stir until simmering, about 5 minutes. Season with salt and black pepper to taste.

Nutrition Information

- Calories: 155 calories
- Total Fat: 5.2 g
- Cholesterol: 10 mg
- Sodium: 451 mg
- Total Carbohydrate: 28.2 g
- Protein: 3.8 g

Sweet Potato Zucchini Hash

"A simple and sweet treat that packs a lot of flavor. It makes a great alternate breakfast side in place of the standard hash browned potatoes. Try it as a breakfast side with scrambled eggs! Sweet potatoes let off a lot of water as they cook, so it may be necessary to drain the hash before serving."

Serving: 4 | Prep: 10 m | Cook: 10 m | Ready in: 20 m

Ingredients

- 3 tablespoons butter

- 1 sweet potato, peeled and cubed
- 2 tablespoons brown sugar
- 1 zucchini, cut into cubes

Direction

- Melt butter in a skillet over medium heat. Stir sweet potatoes into butter to coat. Add brown sugar and stir until integrated.
- Increase heat to medium-high; cook and stir until brown sugar caramelizes on surface of the sweet potato cubes, 5 to 7 minutes.
- Reduce heat to medium-low. Stir zucchini into the sweet potato mixture; cook and stir until zucchini is tender, 5 to 10 minutes. Drain excess liquid to serve.

Nutrition Information

- Calories: 178 calories
- Total Fat: 8.8 g
- Cholesterol: 23 mg
- Sodium: 72 mg
- Total Carbohydrate: 24.3 g
- Protein: 1.7 g

Swiss Chard Sauteed With Lime

"This quick and delicious Swiss chard recipe can be served as a side dish or as a meal over rice."
Serving: 4 | Prep: 10 m | Cook: 5 m | Ready in: 15 m

Ingredients

- 1 bunch Swiss chard, stems and leaves separated

- 3 tablespoons extra-virgin olive oil, divided
- 1/2 teaspoon kosher salt
- 1/2 lime

Direction

- Chop the chard stems into 1/2-inch pieces. Stack the chard leaves, roll them tightly into a cylinder, and chop into 1/2-inch strips; chop the strips into halves.
- Heat about half the olive oil in a large non-stick skillet over medium heat. Cook chopped chard stems in hot oil until hot, about 1 minute. Stir the chard leaves with the stems; cook and stir together 1 minutes more. Drizzle remaining olive oil over the mixture and stir to coat. Continue cooking and stirring until the leaves are nearly wilted, 4 to 5 minutes. Remove from heat and immediately sprinkle kosher salt and squeeze lime half over the chard. Stir to season evenly.

Nutrition Information

- Calories: 104 calories
- Total Fat: 10.3 g
- Cholesterol: 0 mg
- Sodium: 361 mg
- Total Carbohydrate: 3 g
- Protein: 1.1 g

Tampa Coconut Cilantro Rice

"This is a Kerala (Southern India) rendition of coconut rice. It's a tad sweeter than regular rice which cuts through much of the spice found in an accompaniment of a spicy curry such as chicken curry."

Serving: 4 | Prep: 5 m | Cook: 15 m | Ready in: 25 m

Ingredients

- 2 cups coconut water, or as needed
- 1 cup basmati rice
- salt, or as desired
- 1 1/2 tablespoons chopped fresh cilantro
- 2 teaspoons unsalted butter

Direction

- Bring 1 cup coconut water to a boil in a saucepan. Add basmati rice and salt, cover, and reduce heat to simmer. Stir occasionally, adding more coconut water as needed, until rice is soft but not mushy, about 15 minutes.
- Remove rice from heat, stir in cilantro and butter, and cover again. Let stand until coconut water is absorbed and flavors have blended, about 5 minutes more.

Nutrition Information

- Calories: 205 calories
- Total Fat: 2.7 g
- Cholesterol: 5 mg
- Sodium: 708 mg
- Total Carbohydrate: 41.3 g
- Protein: 4.4 g

Tasty Barbecued Asparagus

"A delicious addition to any meal!"
Serving: 4 | Prep: 5 m | Cook: 5 m | Ready in: 10 m
Ingredients

- 1/2 pound fresh asparagus spears, trimmed
- 2 tablespoons sesame oil
- 5 tablespoons soy sauce

Direction

- Preheat an outdoor grill for medium-high heat and lightly oil the grate.
- Place asparagus in a deep casserole dish; evenly coat with sesame oil and soy sauce.
- Cook marinated asparagus on grill until tender, brushing often with marinade, 5 to 10 minutes.

Nutrition Information

- Calories: 82 calories
- Total Fat: 6.9 g
- Cholesterol: 0 mg
- Sodium: 1129 mg
- Total Carbohydrate: 3.7 g
- Protein: 2.5 g

Tempeh Bacon

"Easiest way to prepare tempeh. Pile it on a BLT (or, more accurately, a TLT). Even non-vegetarians will (maybe) like this. Soy sauce can be used in place of tamari if desired. Stores well in a covered container in the refrigerator."

Serving: 4 | Prep: 10 m | Cook: 5 m | Ready in: 15 m

Ingredients

- 1 tablespoon vegetable oil, or more as needed
- 1 (8 ounce) package tempeh, cut into 1/8-inch thick strips
- 2 dashes tamari, or more to taste

Direction

- Heat oil in a skillet over medium heat. Cook tempeh in the hot oil until browned, 2 to 3 minutes per side. Drizzle tamari over cooked tempeh.

Nutrition Information

- Calories: 138 calories
- Total Fat: 9.5 g
- Cholesterol: 0 mg
- Sodium: 33 mg
- Total Carbohydrate: 5.3 g
- Protein: 10.4 g

The Perfect Egyptian Rice With Vermicelli

"Egyptian rice is a very short grain rice, grown in Egypt. It is not cooked the same way as medium or long grain rice. When cooked, it is supposed to have a fluffy texture, not at all sticky."
Serving: 3 | Prep: 10 m | Cook: 21 m | Ready in: 36 m
Ingredients

- 1 1/2 tablespoons olive oil
- 1/4 cup 1/2-inch long vermicelli
- 1 cup Egyptian rice (short-grain rice)
- salt to taste
- 1 3/4 cups water

Direction

- Heat oil in a saucepan over medium heat. Add vermicelli; cook, stirring constantly, until golden brown, 3 to 5 minutes. Remove from heat. Pour in rice and salt; stir until coated with oil.
- Reduce heat to low. Cook the rice mixture, stirring constantly, until rice turns pasty white, 3 to 5 minutes.
- Bring water to a boil in a saucepan.
- Stir water into the rice mixture. Cover; cook until most of the water is absorbed, 10 to 15 minutes. Turn off heat; let sit until remaining water is absorbed, about 5 minutes. Fluff rice with a fork.

Nutrition Information

- Calories: 330 calories
- Total Fat: 7.3 g

- Cholesterol: 0 mg
- Sodium: 57 mg
- Total Carbohydrate: 59.1 g
- Protein: 5.5 g

Twicebaked Cauliflower

"This vegetarian and onion-free version of the dish turned out delicious. Even my cauliflower-hating wife loved it! Served with fresh cracked pepper brought the flavors out nicely."
Serving: 6 | Prep: 15 m | Cook: 35 m | Ready in: 50 m
Ingredients

- 1 large head cauliflower, cut into florets with stems cut into bite-size pieces
- 1 cup shredded Cheddar cheese, divided
- 1/2 cup reduced-fat sour cream
- 4 ounces reduced-fat cream cheese, softened
- 1/4 cup grated Parmesan cheese

Direction

- Preheat oven to 350 degrees F (175 degrees C).
- Place a steamer insert into a saucepan and fill with water to just below the bottom of the steamer. Bring water to a boil. Add cauliflower, cover, and steam until very tender, about 5 minutes.
- Transfer cauliflower to a bowl and mash with a potato masher until few chunks remain; add 1/2 cup Cheddar cheese, sour cream, cream cheese, and Parmesan cheese and mix thoroughly. Spread the mixture into an 8-inch

square casserole dish; top with remaining Cheddar cheese. Cover dish with aluminum foil or lid.
- Bake in preheated oven until hot and bubbling, 20 to 25 minutes. Remove cover and continue baking until the top is browned, about 10 minutes more.

Nutrition Information

- Calories: 196 calories
- Total Fat: 13.1 g
- Cholesterol: 41 mg
- Sodium: 274 mg
- Total Carbohydrate: 10 g
- Protein: 11.3 g

Who Hash

"This super easy dish was one we often had while camping as kids. My sister and I loved it. Many years later, I was challenged to come up with a dish to bring to my sister's for Christmas brunch. I was inspired and made our camper's hash. To justify this humble dish's appearance at Christmas, I called it 'Who Hash,' and a tradition was born. We must have it EVERY Christmas morning. The name of this dish came from a line in Dr. Seuss' 'How the Grinch Stole Christmas' where it is described that the Grinch stole everything in the Who's house, 'the Grinch even took their last can of Who hash.'"

Serving: 4 | Prep: 5 m | Cook: 15 m | Ready in: 20 m

Ingredients

- 1 tablespoon vegetable oil

- 2 (15 ounce) cans diced white potatoes, drained
- 1 (12 ounce) can fully cooked luncheon meat (such as SPAM®), diced
- 1/2 onion, chopped

Direction

- Heat oil in a non-stick skillet over medium heat. Spread potatoes and meat in a single layer into the skillet; cook until browned on the bottom, about 5 minutes. Turn potatoes and meat to cook other side until browned, about 5 minutes more. Stir onion into the potato mixture; cook and stir until the onion is tender, 5 to 7 minutes.

Nutrition Information

- Calories: 405 calories
- Total Fat: 26.8 g
- Cholesterol: 60 mg
- Sodium: 1657 mg
- Total Carbohydrate: 27.7 g
- Protein: 14.3 g

Wilted Collards

"This is a very good recipe for people who do not like collard greens. Collards may be cooked ahead and re-heated. Serve with hot pepper vinegar if desired."

Serving: 6 | Prep: 15 m | Cook: 20 m | Ready in: 35 m

Ingredients

- 1/2 pound bacon, diced

- 2 bunches collard greens, trimmed and chopped
- 1 large onion, chopped
- 2 cloves garlic, minced
- 1 tablespoon white sugar

Direction

- Place bacon in a large, deep pot; cook and stir over medium-high heat until evenly browned, about 10 minutes. Cook and stir collard greens, onion, garlic, and sugar into the cooked bacon. Cover pot and let mixture steam until collard greens are wilted, 3 to 4 minutes. Remove cover, raise heat to high, and cook until liquid is evaporated, about 5 minutes.

Nutrition Information

- Calories: 114 calories
- Total Fat: 5.6 g
- Cholesterol: 14 mg
- Sodium: 305 mg
- Total Carbohydrate: 10.2 g
- Protein: 7.2 g

Yum Yum Cranberry Salad

"Yum, yum; enjoy. Keep chilled until ready to serve. This is better when it's made the night before enjoying."
Serving: 6 | Prep: 15 m | Cook: 5 m | Ready in: 20 m

Ingredients

- 1 (12 ounce) package fresh cranberries
- 1 1/2 cups white sugar

- 1 (8 ounce) can crushed pineapple, drained
- 1/4 cup pecans, or to taste
- 2 pints heavy whipping cream

Direction

- Blend cranberries in a food processor until ground; pour into a large bowl.
- Pour sugar evenly over the top of the cranberries. Spread pineapple over the sugar layer; add pecans.
- Pour whipping cream into a bowl; beat until stiff peaks form. Fold the whipped cream into the cranberry mixture until ingredients are evenly mixed.

Nutrition Information

- Calories: 823 calories
- Total Fat: 62.4 g
- Cholesterol: 217 mg
- Sodium: 62 mg
- Total Carbohydrate: 67.8 g
- Protein: 4.1 g

Yummy Grilled Asparagus

"I created this last summer. It goes great with all grilled meats and fish."

Serving: 4 | Prep: 10 m | Cook: 10 m | Ready in: 20 m

Ingredients

- 1 bunch fresh asparagus, trimmed

- 1/3 cup Italian-style dressing (such as Bernstein's Restaurant Recipe®)
- 3/4 teaspoon lemon pepper
- salt and ground black pepper to taste

Direction

- Preheat grill for medium heat and lightly oil the grate.
- Lay asparagus flat in a 9x9-inch pan. Add Italian dressing, lemon pepper, salt, and black pepper; toss to coat. Transfer asparagus using tongs to the grill.
- Grill asparagus on preheated grill until tender, 3 to 5 minutes per side. Return asparagus to pan and toss with remaining dressing mixture.

Nutrition Information

- Calories: 80 calories
- Total Fat: 5.7 g
- Cholesterol: 0 mg
- Sodium: 413 mg
- Total Carbohydrate: 6.5 g
- Protein: 2.6 g

Zesty Kale

"This quick and easy recipe makes an excellent side dish with lots of flavor. I became intrigued by kale after having it served to me twice in the past two weeks. My wife and I really enjoyed my new and zesty creation."

Serving: 2 | Prep: 10 m | Ready in: 10 m

Ingredients

- 4 teaspoons reduced-sodium soy sauce
- 1 teaspoon toasted sesame oil
- 1 1/2 teaspoons minced garlic
- 4 leaves kale, stems removed and discarded, leaves torn into bite-sized pieces

Direction

- Whisk soy sauce, sesame oil, and garlic together in a bowl.
- Place kale leaves in a bowl; drizzle soy sauce dressing over kale. Toss to coat.

Nutrition Information

- Calories: 50 calories
- Total Fat: 2.7 g
- Cholesterol: 0 mg
- Sodium: 372 mg
- Total Carbohydrate: 5.6 g
- Protein: 2 g

CPSIA information can be obtained
at www.ICGtesting.com
Printed in the USA
BVHW071938200421
605395BV00004B/475